A Parent's Guide To Prayer

ANITA E. KEIRE

Curriculum Development Associates, Inc.
28 Old Boston Post Road
Old Saybrook, CT 06475
(203) 388-6878

ISBN 0-9633911-0-0
Library of Congress Catalog Card No. 92-073106

Illustrations by Isabelle McDonnell
Cover by Bette S. Baker

Acknowledgments

✻

Special thanks are due several people who have read and offered helpful advice at various phases of the creation of this book. I am grateful to Margaret and William Berg, John Donovan, Mark Carruthers, Barbara Brodbeck, Betty Durland, Linda and Donald Ferrier, Laurel Friedmann, Cora Hokunson, Susan Howell, Myrna and Bruce Kamens, Mara Keire, Virginia King, Nancy Millen, Sara Rawson, Walter Wagoner, and Bonnie Woit. I thank them for their time, their constructive criticism, and their honesty with me.

This book is dedicated to my husband, Fred, who has been deprived of my time and has encouraged me to press forward when discouraged, and to Betty Durland, my business partner, who has worked unselfishly for the last two years to further the cause of Christian education in the United States.

Other works by Anita E. Keire

*

Mustard Seed Series, Christian Education Curriculum

To Fred, my dear, patient husband

and

To Betty, a very special friend.

Contents

✳

Earth's crammed with heaven,
And every common bush afire with God;
But only he who sees takes off his shoes;
The rest sit round it and pluck blackberries.
                    Elizabeth Barrett Browning

1

*

Introduction

The dogwood tree outside my window is dripping with little droplets of water. It is the beginning of March. All winter long I have looked at this dogwood tree while writing this book. For years, it has been my silent writing companion. Its branches give birds a perch on which to sing their song. In the fall, the squirrels go out on its farthest limbs to gather up its berries. This tree gives me shade in the summer and allows the sun to shine through in the winter. The joy it has given me is unforgettable.

This book, like the dogwood tree, can serve as a companion to you in your life cycle as a parent and teacher in guiding your children's spiritual journey. An important part of that spiritual journey is prayer. I hope my knowledge, experiences, and understanding of my spiritual journey—parts of which I am about to share with you—will benefit you and your children. I was raised in a religious home where form and ritual took the place of discussing our Christian story and the living out of our faith. My family shunned my faith questions.

When I was eleven, my mother died after three years of fighting lung cancer. I was relieved for my mother because she could not suffer any more no matter how much she may have loved us and wanted to be with us. Friends tried to comfort us. Various well-meaning people suggested that my mother was too good to live on earth, therefore, God called her home. Others suggested that she had to suffer to purify her soul so that she could go to heaven. I was unable to accept any of the reasons given to me.

What nagged me most was: why did God let my mother become sick and die? Why did God not perform a miracle and let her live? Did God not hear our prayers?

As a consequence of the trauma of my mother's illness and death, I have spent a lifetime on a spiritual quest. The journey has been difficult, treacherous, hindered by some, and has gone down many roads that led nowhere. This quest began with an immature faith, struggled through many doubts, and eventually led to an enduring faith and trust in God. Answers to many of my questions still remain unanswered and may never be answered. But now I am able to live with the limited knowledge and experience God permits me to have.

From my conversations with other Christians, my spiritual needs and quest are theirs, too. Maybe your spiritual journey, which is also reflected in your prayer life, has been as bumpy as mine. Many of us have grasped at bits and pieces of information and enlightenment to help us understand what is happening to us and those around us in the journey of life. Many of us have been too tentative in passing on to children what we know and believe about God and prayer, thereby impoverishing their spiritual lives.

This book is written for parents and teachers as a resource and reference aid for understanding prayer that will in turn help you guide your children's spiritual journey and prayer life.

Dr. Elisabeth Kubler-Ross, a pioneer working in death, dying, and healing, has suggested that there are four quadrants that shape the whole person. These are the physical, intellectual, spiritual, and emotional quadrants. Each quadrant interpenetrates the other and needs adequate development in order for a whole child to emerge. If one quadrant remains undeveloped, it is as though one of the four foundational pillars that support a house was not built to the height of the other pillars, thus making the house vulnerable to collapse in the first big storm.

I will concentrate mostly on the spiritual quadrant and most notably on prayer. The other three quadrants will also influence the spiritual side of our being. If we favor one quadrant at the expense of the others, I believe we create an imbalance in our lives and ultimately some form of illness.

This book focuses on questions children, adults, and I have asked at one time or another about prayer and the rationale behind the answers to these questions. This book is my gift to you in helping you and your children in the spiritual journey of life. As the birds alight on the branches of my dogwood tree, so may you choose to use this book for a time. Then you may find some other branch in some other tree that may be more to your liking and need.

In the meantime, keep this book by your bed. Read it from time to time. Read it slowly and as often as you wish. Use it as a reference book, a home aid in developing your and your children's spiritual lives to which you can refer when you have questions. Definitions for terms frequently used will have one asterisk* after the term and will be found in the glossary at the end of the book.

You may write me through my publisher if you have any questions not addressed in this book and if you have contributions and experiences which you wish to share with me and a wider audience. From this information, I may write a sequel.

When Moses threw the wand into the Red Sea, the sea, quite contrary to the expected miracle, did not divide itself to leave a dry passage for the Jews. Not until the first man had jumped into the sea did the promised miracle happen and the waves recede.

Jewish legend

2

✳

What Is Prayer?

The first and perhaps the most important step in overcoming my sense of inadequacy regarding prayer began when I developed an understanding of what prayer is. Most of this understanding came to me through my study of scripture. I have come to the conclusion that prayer consists of at least the following:

1. *Prayer expresses our faith that God exists, that God is accessible to us, and that we can be aware of God's presence.* If we do not believe in God's existence and presence, our prayers are meaningless. Our prayers will not be directed to God and are nothing more than a conversation with ourselves. For God to *be* God to us, we must believe that God is the Supreme Being upon whom we and all creation depend and with whom a trusting and familiar relationship can exist.

2. *Prayer is communication between God and us.* Prayer is our turning to a higher power. Prayer is built on the raw material of life: our joys, sorrows, hopes, successes, defeats, loves, fears, needs, and emotions. We bring to God all that is in our hearts

---

and on our minds. Our denials and our disguises are dropped
in God's presence. We are our true selves. The psalmist said it
best:

> O Lord, you have searched me and known me.
> You know when I sit down and when I rise up;
> you discern my thoughts from far away.
> You search out my path and my lying down,
> and are acquainted with all my ways.

Psalm 139:1-3[**]

The saying of set prayers and petitions to God dominated
my early prayer life. They did not seem to connect me with
God. These set prayers made me feel like a school girl reciting
a memorized poem to God. They were not the real me speaking to God. And, because of my mother's early death, I did not
believe God wanted to hear my petitions. I was never encouraged to say what was in my heart, nor did I wish to expose to
others my deepest thoughts. For far too long I conformed to
the expectations of those around me by saying other people's
prayers.

In time, I came to understand that God cares most about our
attitudes and feelings, not set prayer recitals. Jesus taught us
that we can approach God as intimately and securely as a little
child approaches a beloved parent (Matthew 19:13-15). I believe what Jesus taught. I believe God is endowed with certain
human characteristics such as feelings of love, pain, and
thought which make possible a relationship to exist between
God and us. We might say, therefore, that most prayer comes
from the depth of our hearts and souls. It cannot be governed
by rules and prescriptions. Nonetheless, I have come to appreciate the place in prayer for reading, meditating upon, and saying the simple and the great prayers that have been given to us
through past and present generations of believers. These
prayers teach us other people's understanding of God and in-

[**]All Bible quotations are from the New Oxford Annotated Bible with
the Apocrypha, New Revised Standard Version.

spire us to identify with them in exploring and developing our relationship with God.

3. *Prayer is complete attention to God. It is a form of listening.* God need not speak to us in words. God speaks to us through other people, events in life, nature, the promptings of the Holy Spirit, and scripture. Jesus indirectly revealed to us much about the personality of God through His parables. He often said to His disciples: "He who has ears to hear, let him hear" (Mark 4:9). Through intense listening we can hear and come to understand what God is saying to us.

I pray on the principle that wine knocks the cork out of a bottle. There is an inward fermentation, and there must be a vent.

Henry Ward Beecher

3

✳

What Motivates Us to Pray?

Children will ask us why we pray or why they should pray. What follows are some reasons we can give them.

God creates within us the desire to pray. Prayer is a natural response to God who made our world. Prayer begins when we are little children. When we see the beauty of the world, some of us stop and thank God for the wonders we behold in nature and science. We praise God for the orderly rhythm of the seasons, of day and night, and of sunshine and of rain. The ravages of hurricanes, blizzards, and earthquakes frighten us. They tell us we are not fully in control of God's universe. God is. God is our magnificent Creator whom Jesus taught us we should approach with love, reverence, and gratitude.

We seek greater knowledge of God and desire a relationship with God. We wonder what life is all about. We talk to God about our lives, about the direction we are taking, and question whether this direction is what God has planned for us. We listen to, study, and act upon God's word and will as it is revealed to us through scripture and everyday events. We meditate and reflect on God's word and movement among us. We ask God to help us by revealing the spiritual significance of what we have heard, read, received, and experienced.

In our loneliness and despair, we can turn to God and find God with open arms to comfort us, to give us the love and assurance we need. Often we are like children who skin their knees and run crying to their mother for sympathy, a hug, and a kiss. As adults, however, our hurts, sufferings, and pain are not so easily relieved. Usually they are far greater, deeper, and more trying than those of children. We try to change the course of tragic events in our lives and in the lives of our children but cannot always do so. Prayer helps sustain us.

Continual prayer builds a trusting and familiar relationship between God and ourselves. We are not strangers to each other. Because of this relationship, we are open to God's presence and know that we are never alone. We know God cares for us and is with us under the most trying circumstances to give us the confidence and courage we need.

We often seek from God material improvement in our lives. We want God to make it possible for us to earn more money, to win prizes, and to gain the positions we seek. We may rationalize that what we seek from God will be for the welfare of our families and society as well as for ourselves and therefore is not selfish. Our motives behind certain prayers are often for our own self-advancement and not in accord with God's will*. And what is God's will? There is no one definition for it, but it runs like a red thread throughout the Bible. God's will is unity, peace, wholeness, joy, goodness, righteousness, purity, fidelity, love, hope, and faithfulness. I will address this issue more fully throughout this book.

We also come to God in prayer with the sins that unsettle our souls and create walls between God, ourselves, and others. We come to God asking for forgiveness and for strength to avoid future sins. We ask God to help us seek and obtain forgiveness from those against whom we have sinned. We know that God forgives those who are truly sorry for the evil they have caused and who seek to live the future according to God's rule in their lives.

Because God has been good to us, we love and pray to God that we may spend eternity with God. Through our faith in Jesus, we have hope and have reason to believe that this prayer will be answered.

Lastly, we pray to God for *shalom** (peace). God's *shalom* means freedom from internal and external conflict, from unjust barriers between people. *Shalom* is the experience of God's grace and tranquillity of heart. Though wars and conflicts may not cease in our lifetime, God will help us withstand these distresses and will give us the peace that passes all understanding which the world can neither give to us nor take away.

In prayer, we lift up our hearts, our minds, and our souls to God who actively moves towards us. Prayer is the continuance of this loving relationship between our Creator and us.

I have been driven many times to my knees by the overwhelming conviction that I had nowhere else to go.

Abraham Lincoln

4

*

Why Teach Children to Pray?

As parents and teachers, we try to expose our children to the best possible influences that will help shape and define them. What we say and do will have an impact on them and their future as adults. There are two different dominant life styles, norms, and values they can adopt. One style is governed by the dominant culture and the other by the religious life and more specifically the Christian life.

Throughout the centuries, the dominant culture has always favored those people who are attracted to and participate in the tantalizing temptations that position, wealth, and power create. These temptations create an elitist mentality that requires conformity to a group's norms which often oppress those who accept them as well as those who do not. Children need to learn the difference between God's will* and a group's norms opposed to God's will. For example, children need to learn that power, wealth, and position can be abused through hate tactics of one group against another as found in racism,

---

bigotry, and religious intolerance. Abuse of power, wealth, and position often occurs when a person has been given or believes he** has preferential rights over other people. This power may be corrupted by predatory behavior that influences the psychological, sexual, economic, legal, military, and physical dimension of life. People with great resources have the potential for abusing those with less.

Christians, who are followers of Christ, find their faith which shapes their values and conduct vulnerable to the dominant culture's social norms. Young people often are seduced by non-Christian values. We play an important part in helping children develop the tools and knowledge to step outside of the "ethical context" created by society. We have to help children develop a clear self-definition and understanding of whom they are. They need to know they are God's children, that God's will should rule their lives, and that they should not willingly conform to a group's norms unless these norms are in accordance with God's will. For these reasons, we need to teach our children to communicate with God through prayer so they are connected to the Source of life that will give them the strength and courage for their journey in life. They need to learn that God's love is unconditional and that God's will is non-negotiable. If children elect to be disciples of Jesus, who is God incarnate, then the behavior and motivation needs to be aligned with God's will*. Often Jesus may be the *only* one with whom they can talk. Jesus is their best friend and was tempted like they. They can tell Him anything, and He will listen and love them. Children's lives and their choices are not easy today. They need Jesus' friendship, communication with Him, and the knowledge that being a Christian is part of their identity.

If they love Jesus, He challenges them to carry on His work and make whatever sacrifices in their lives necessary to bring good news to the poor, release to the captives, recovery of sight to the blind, and liberation to the oppressed (Luke 4:18).

**Masculine language and pronouns used in this book are gender neutral and apply to both genders.

Love and *dedication* to their tasks of caring for others is what Jesus requires of them. If they are to follow Him, they are to give life to others. This concept of giving life to others is very difficult for young children to understand. Adolescents have a better understanding of this concept and can willingly make their decisions whether to follow Jesus and adhere to God's will or be coopted by the dominant culture and its values.

Children eventually become adults and the cycle of passing on the faith repeats itself. Our particular faith story and experiences can influence each other and our children. What I am about to tell you is one such story that tells us about the positive value of prayer.

Not too long ago, I happened to meet an old friend I had not seen in a long time. Years ago we took turns driving our daughters to ballet classes and Brownies. Until this recent meeting, I did not know that she had another daughter. This beautiful girl has a severe and rare neurological disorder that impairs her physical agility and mental dexterity. My friend has placed her career on hold. She devotes most of her energies to helping her daughter.

I ran into her in the library researching all available literature on her daughter's condition. She wishes to prepare herself and her daughter for the future. She had heard that I had become a minister, and she poured out her concern, her love, and her hope for a continuation of the little miracles that have occurred over the years with this daughter.

We decided to have lunch together before parting. At lunch we discussed her and her daughter's situation further. Her daughter's fierce determination motivates her to be like other children. I told her about a deaf young woman I knew, of how her mother never gave up on her, how the school personnel helped her achieve great things within her limitations, and how this girl has become an outstanding, exceptional woman. But more importantly, this friend and her daughter learned the real lesson to quit trying to be "normal" according to society's standards. She is loved by God and by her family just as she is. She quit trying to be like everyone else. She is living her life in terms of possibilities rather than being governed by limitations. I suggested to my friend that she and her daughter do likewise.

Then my friend said to me. "You know, I have been so discouraged recently and was not sure what to do next. I prayed for God's help. During my prayers I felt as though Jesus were encouraging me to turn over this great load to Him. And I did. Then I felt at peace. I have been trying to live one day at a time. I know our love for our daughter will sustain us. But you know what, Anita, I think somehow we were meant to meet each other today. I needed to be with you and to hear about this special young woman and how she is making her way in life."

In the conclusion of John's gospel, Jesus questions Peter three times whether he loves Him. Each time Peter answers: "Yes, Lord; you know that I love you." Finally, Jesus instructs Peter and by association all Christians to:

> Feed my sheep. Very truly, I tell you, when you were younger, you used to fasten your own belt and to go wherever you wished. But when you grow old, you will stretch out your hands, and someone else will fasten a belt around you and take you where you do not wish to go....Follow me.
>
> John 21:18-19

When we were children, most of us were carefree with someone else taking care of our needs. In time, we learned to take responsibility for our lives. We made decisions that have brought us to where we are today. Now that we are adults, Jesus is asking us to follow Him and to be open and giving vessels of Jesus' love. We have been given the sacred trust to feed and tend spiritually those children in our care. Part of that sacred trust is spiritual guidance in prayer.

Let me live in my house by the side of the road
Where the race of men go by;
They are good, they are bad, they are weak,
they are strong,
Wise, foolish—so am I.
Then why should I sit in the scorner's seat,
Or hurl the cynic's ban?
Let me live in my house by the side of the road
And be a friend of man.

Sam Walter Foss
The House by the Side of the Road

❋

Two roads diverged in a wood, and I—
I took the one less traveled by,
And that has made all the difference.

Robert Frost
The Road Not Taken

5

*

How Can I Guide Children in Prayer?

Whether we like it or not, we are our children's role model and spiritual leader. Given our limitations, how are we going to help them along their spiritual journey? First, it is important to know and understand as much of the process as is possible. Second, growth in the spirit is through knowledge of God and the workings of the Holy Spirit together with our guidance and assistance. What follows are some important processes to keep in mind as you accompany your children on their spiritual journey.

Our spiritual journey takes us into uncharted territory. Part of that spiritual journey leads us to establishing an important relationship with God. We learn to trust God and to go into the dark unknown with the faith that God is with us.

We are all at different places in our spiritual journey. Each step of the journey takes its own time. God knows where we are and who we are. The process cannot be hurried. We and our children's spiritual lives are like a grain of mustard seed which Jesus compares to the Kingdom of God. The mustard seed, "when sown upon the ground, is the smallest of all the seeds on earth; yet when it is sown it grows up and becomes the greatest of all shrubs, and puts forth large branches, so that the birds of the air can make nests in its shade" (Mark 4:31-32).

Somehow spiritual growth occurs. From such small beginnings, Jesus and His disciples then and now have brought the Kingdom of God* into our midst. The Kingdom of God is any place where people live according to God's will. It has its start here on earth and its completion in heaven*. The contrast between the grain of mustard seed to the Kingdom of God in the grown mustard shrub is so great as to suggest that this miracle and mystery is possible only when God is active in the process.

The Kingdom of God grows within us in mysterious ways. God's kingdom remains lowly like the mustard seed shrub. Its lowliness is its power. Its perpetuation depends on our planting and the giving of physical, intellectual, emotional, and spiritual space and fertilization so that the seedlings which are planted can grow and mature. We are like the farmer who plows the field, sows seeds, weeds, and waters them. Once we have done our work, we have to trust and leave the rest to God.

An enduring faith grows out of knowledge of God. An enduring faith does not grow out of ignorant piety. Knowledge of God begins with us and expands with a comprehensive, systematic building-block approach to Christian education that studies God's actions and revelations in scripture and in current affairs. Christian education attempts to educate children to a Christian view of life.

John Calvin criticized ignorant piety when he said in his *Institutes, III, 2, 2-3:*

Is this what believing means—to understand nothing, provided only that you submit your feeling obediently to the Church? Faith rests not on ignorance, but on knowledge. We do not obtain salvation either because we are prepared to embrace as true whatever the Church has prescribed, or because we turn over to it the task of inquiry and knowing...It would be the height of absurdity to label ignorance tempered by humility "faith"!

Additionally, Calvin warns us to examine and consider what we receive as truth "for it is not possible...that perfect knowledge should break forth at once." In essence, Calvin is suggesting we avoid teaching our children a reductionist knowledge of the faith where everything is reduced to a few simple truths. Faith and true knowledge of God are a lifelong endeavor. If we persist on our journey, God gives us glimpses and spiritual insights as to what God is all about. Those glimpses are similar to a shade being raised to let the light in for a short time and then being lowered again. Sometimes we see and understand and sometimes we do not.

Spiritual journeys last an eternity. The baggage of things and events can weigh us down, distract us, and diminish the importance and purpose of our journey. God gives us the gift of time to fill our lives to the brim to be used to further God's kingdom.

If we travel through life in God's presence, we need to come as we are and not behind masks. Only openness, honesty, humility, and sincerity are acceptable to God (see the parable of the Pharisee and Publican, Luke 18:9-14). To pray and to journey with God means we are willing for change to occur within us. This transformation will cause us to look upon life from God's perspective. Christ's light will then shine through us.

Prayer is our faith speaking. We are to be like a living, fruitful tree planted next to the water of life, the source of our strength. We will be known by our fruit.

Prayer is a very personal matter. We and our children have different personalities, means of self expression, maturity, knowledge, and understanding of God and these will determine the level and kind of communication we have with God. For instance, the young child may feel God's presence but may not understand its meaning. Adults may have an intellectual understanding of God but may not experience God's presence.

Prayer is our private, innermost communication with God. Nobody else is privy to that communication except when we join together in communal prayer. Even then the assembled faith community will not know in what direction God may be leading each one of us. Therefore, when introducing prayer and guiding children in prayer, remember there are no set rules, regulations, and techniques for prayer. Our prayer lives and that of our children need to be respected and not violated. Their prayer lives need to be allowed to develop according to their individual personalities and learning styles.

Privacy is important. Privacy does not mean and should not mean that we cannot talk to children about prayer and pray with them. Prayer is private but not a secret. We can best teach our children by setting an example.

Prayer is part of our spiritual journey together. As parents we are aware of the mystery and wonder of the newborn baby we have held in our arms. Our children connect us with past generations, our present generation, and with future generations. Our children connect us with each other and with God. In fact, for many of us, it is because of our children that we have returned to God since they help us realize that all of life is sacred.

We may feel inadequate and uncomfortable assuming responsibility for our children's spiritual lives. Perhaps we are inadequate and our prayer lives may be inadequate. But we have to do our best. If we fail to meet their basic needs, who else will have as much heartfelt concern for their spiritual well-being? I believe we cannot shift this burden to the church entirely. At best, most churches only have our children for a mere thirty hours a year for religious instruction or the equivalent to one week of schooling. Development of our children's spiritual lives has to be a mutually cooperative effort between the church and home with the principal responsibility residing with the parents.

Our fears and disappointments about prayer may discourage us. We need to let go of them and let down our defenses. If we ask, God will help us. Nothing is impossible for God, and we have the confidence that God hears us. Ask God for help and guidance in helping us to overcome obstacles to prayer in our own lives as well as in our children's.

Look upon our willingness to help develop our children's prayer lives as God's way of coaxing those of us who have been separated from God to reestablish the relationship we once had but somehow lost because of turbulence in our teen and early adult years or because of some traumatic experience. Parents and Sunday school teachers must assume their role as spiritual leaders of their children.

Life is a physical, emotional, intellectual, and spiritual journey which we all have to make. Our physical journeys from birth to death progress at a given pace over which we have little control. Usually our intellectual journeys are very deliberate. We decide early in life what we wish to become when we grow up. We educate and train ourselves for our life's chosen work. At various times, we place too much emphasis on success and little or no emphasis on spiritual growth. When we are emotionally and spiritually immature, we let our friends and society determine our self-image. We accept their evaluation of our relative success or failure. Too often our culture fails to value our inner and spiritual lives. By definition, secular society values the material over the spiritual, the visible over the invisible. Yet our society wonders why our people, especially our young people, are so troubled and seem cast adrift.

It is important that we and our children know where we are going and what we want to achieve in life. A visit to a cemetery with them, especially an old one, might be a good experience. Read the epitaphs on the gravestones. Discuss them and their possible meaning. Together try to imagine what the lives of the people buried there must have been like. Let our children make up stories about the different lives represented there. Then consider the ideals by which we will best be remembered. Will people remember us as good or evil? Did we share with others or were we greedy? Did we use the gifts God gave to us to achieve all we could be or did we throw them away? With whom did we travel the journey of life?

Was God a part of that journey? Discuss these ideals and epitaphs without moralizing.

Some of us may live and die believing we failed in nurturing our children in the Christian faith. Some of our parents believed this about us. Here is a story Alexander Macleod told his congregation at the beginning of this century. He said:

> In a small village, there once lived a godly man with a wife and three sons. His wife died and the job of rearing his three sons fell on him. He cried to God to help him. Now, it so happened that in that house there was a rush-bottomed chair, the only chair of that sort in the house, and it was at that chair this man knelt when he prayed for his boys as well as at family prayer. Often, when alone, this man prayed for the conversion of his sons. But he saw no change in his sons; they were hard, selfish, and worldly. At last one by one they all left him, and went into business in some great city of the land. They prospered in business, but not in faith. Business prosperity brought them no joy and made them hard. Then the father prayed the more earnestly that they might gain their own souls, although they should lose the whole world. But at the end of his days they were unchanged. There was an old servant who lived in the house, and to her he said when he was dying, "I will pray now that my death may be used by God to save them." Then he died.
>
> The three young men came home to the funeral. And when all was past, they said: "What shall we do with the house and the old furniture?" One said: "Let them go to the old woman who has taken care of him." But the eldest son said: "Well, I consent if only you will allow me to keep the rush-bottomed chair. I never heard prayers like those I heard there. I hear those prayers still when I am at business. I think if I had the chance I would not live the prayerless life I am living now." And with that the eldest brother said: "Let us kneel around the old chair once more and pray." And they did. And with great crying and tears they spent that afternoon together. By the end of the day, the two younger brothers decided to give up their businesses and to become missionaries. The eldest brother decided to return to church and be a lay leader in it.[1]

For true prayer to begin, we need to understand the process, to stop keeping God at arm's length, to pray, and to encourage our children to have interaction with God. Prayer is attention to God. Prayer is journeying through life with God.

It is in knowledge as in swimming; he who flounders and splashes on the surface, makes more noise, and attracts more attention than the pearl-diver who quietly dives in quest of treasures to the bottom.

Washington Irving

*

A little kingdom I possess,
   Where thoughts and feelings dwell;
And very hard the task I find
   Of governing it well.
. . . .
I do not ask for any crown
   But that which all may win;
Nor try to conquer any world
   Except the one within....

Louisa May Alcott

6

＊

What Lessons Can We Learn from the Lord's Prayer?

The Lord's Prayer has an interesting history. Early Christians held the Lord's Prayer in reverence and awe. It was first taught to Jesus' disciples as a model prayer for their prayer lives. In the early church, the Lord's Prayer was first taught to the newly baptized as part of the church's tradition for teaching and interpretation of the Christian life. The Lord's Prayer can function the same today with our children. Help our children understand what each statement and petition means. Discuss them at length one by one with them over a period of time. Let them suggest possible new interpretations to each petition beyond what is given here and how they relate to their lives.

The opening statement in the Lord's Prayer, *Our father* signifies God as creator of the universe and of us. We belong to

God. God is not only like a parent to each one of us in the faith community but to all peoples in all lands and in all nations. The word *our* teaches us that God belongs to all peoples rather than to a particular religious sect, people, or person. All who come before God come with an equal status to everyone else.

With the words *Our father* we are opening up our presence to the reality and presence of God. We are expressing our relationship to God.

The next petition *Who art in heaven* tells us that God is found in no specific geographic location. Heaven* is not a place in the sky with spatial dimensions. Rather, heaven is a place where we experience God's presence. No church, temple, place, or book can contain God even though God may be present in these locations. Jesus is telling us that where God is heaven is.

Hallowed be thy name means that God's name is above all names. *Hallowed** means holy. Something that is holy is set apart, regarded with awe. To hallow God's name means to regard God's name and God with awe and as the most sacred, holy, valuable name in all the universe.

We come into God's presence thinking about God, allowing God to touch our spirits and our entire lives. We are aware of God's holiness. Without this awareness, true prayer does not exist. The atmosphere of prayer requires a certain reverence and awe.

Not so many years ago my husband and I sailed into Edgartown, Massachusetts. We went ashore, walked through the business district into the residential area. It was 6 p.m. The carillion of the Congregational Church was playing *Jesus Calls Us, O'er the Tumult.* The church was set far back from the road and high up on a hill. We walked up to this church. A few people were there. At that moment, I felt God calling me to forget the activities of life and to a moment of special communion. We were standing on holy ground—ground that had been set aside solely for the worship of God. I could feel God's presence all about me. At that moment God's presence and name were hallowed for me.

Many people have never experienced God's presence and

therefore make fun of those who believe in God and in God's presence. They are too much a part of this world and believe that if they cannot plug into God like they would some machine and get a spurt of energizing power from God that God does not exist. God may not exist for them because they do not give God a chance to be a part of their lives.

The Kingdom of God is not a retreat from the concrete world. When we pray *Thy kingdom come,* we are praying that our little kingdoms and spheres of influence may perish so God's kingdom and rule can be established. Are we and our children ready for God's rule? Do we really want to give up what little power we hold over others and submit to God's will and rule in our lives?

Thy kingdom come is an important statement. Discuss it at length and from various angles with our children, especially junior and senior high school youth. For instance, how do our political, business, medical, religious, and educational leaders perform in their little kingdoms? Whose will dominates them? What motivates them? Are these leaders more interested in preserving their positions or acquiring new positions of power? Or are they interested in helping humankind? What do our children think these people should continue or discontinue doing? How do our leaders use people's emotions or gullibility to achieve the ends they want? What rights are they willing to grant others even though it means they may lose some rights or privileges in order to do God's will? How does bringing in God's kingdom* challenge our very way of relating to the world? What happened to Jesus because people did not want to give up their kingdoms? How do we evaluate the decisions we make for the present moment with those decisions that will effect eternity?

When we say *Thy will be done,* we are responding to Jesus' call for conversion in His announcement of God's Kingdom. Jesus challenges us to turn away from all that rules our lives, be it money, power, technology, or ideology and to turn to God and stand in God's presence. Jesus' call to faith liberates us and frees us from our private agenda. Jesus is asking us to forsake our sins so that we can overcome the wounds our sins have caused and begin the healing process. Jesus asks us to let go of all that prevents our doing God's will, to say "no" to oppression and all that holds us in bondage.

Children need to know that they cannot impose their will on God. Jesus showed us in the Garden of Gethsemane that He was not resigned to God's will. In fact, there was a terrible struggle that went on inside of Jesus. He did not wish to go to the cross. And who among us could blame Him? But He knew that if He ran from the cross, He would be repudiating all that He represented. Therefore, Jesus said, "Not my will, but thy will be done." Jesus submitted His will to God's will. He made a conscious decision to take a stand against the kingdoms of this world.

We, too, as Jesus' disciples, may have to make worldly sacrifices to see that God's kingdom is realized. We may have to give up our little kingdoms. We need to learn to live out our prayers in action and not just in wishful thinking. Where God's will is done, health can be restored to relationships. Peace and love for God and each other can reign. Where God's will is not done, unrest, greed, and self interest destroy God's kingdom.

God's will is to be done *On earth as it is in heaven*. God has entrusted the earth to us. God wishes us to bring our will into conformity with God's will where God's will is lived out and not forced on people. If we live by God's will, we will live in faith, hope, and love. Beginning with ourselves, we will begin to live out the content of heaven.

Give us this day our daily bread. This petition is the central petition of the Lord's Prayer. God's will dominates the first half of the prayer and our needs the second half. This petition addresses our need for spiritual, emotional, mental, and intellectual health as well as for the essentials of life, those things that are necessary for life to exist.

And what are the essentials of life?

God gives us a world rich in food and resources for shelter and clothing. God says it is all ours. How will we use these gifts? God puts us all to the test. Shall we hoard our excess which, like the manna the Jewish people hoarded in the desert, becomes unusable to us? Are we thankful to God for God's gifts? Are we able to share our goods with the needy? Or do we eat our loaf of bread before hungry, needy people? Suggest that our children picture themselves as the one with plenty. What would they do and why? How would they feel and what would they do if they were the needy ones?

How does our willingness or unwillingness to share our plenty speak volumes about our faith, our trust in God, our thankfulness and gratitude or lack of them? If we are willing to share what we have, our action states that we recognize God as the creator and giver of life. How are we making a faith statement? If we withhold our excess from God and the needy, how does this action show that we look to ourselves and not to God for our basic needs and as the source and giver of life? How does the parable of the rich man and Lazarus address the use of God's gifts (Luke 16:19-31)?

One clue to God's intentions is the word *us* in *Give us this day our daily bread.* The word *us* reminds us that we cannot ask for the essentials of life for ourselves alone. We, who are satiated, or full, have a responsibility to be concerned about and share what we have with the rest of the human race. That means that economic and political exploitation that deprives people of the essentials of life should not be tolerated. Why?

Jesus spent a lot of time in table fellowship with those who were considered the marginalized people in His society. His meal time with them symbolized His connectedness with all people both in their bodily needs as well as in their spiritual needs. The Lord's Supper celebrates this table fellowship with Jesus and with one another. Bread and water are symbols for paradise. Bread and water witness to the fullness of God's material and spiritual gifts. They are soul food. Every day life is hallowed* and made holy.

In some ways, Jesus is saying that our spiritual needs are even more important than our physical needs. We need God's help to get us through difficult times. We need to be reassured that God loves us. Those spiritual gifts God has given us are not to be hoarded either. They are meant to be spent daily. Ask our children why our spiritual needs may be more important than our material needs. What does it mean to spend our spiritual gifts? What happens when we do?

And forgive us our debts (trespasses/sins) as we forgive our debtors (those who trespass/sin against us). Our human needs go beyond our need for bread and spiritual sustenance. They also include our need for forgiveness from God and for the act of forgiveness on our part. Why?

The word debt had a strongly religious connotation in Jewish culture 2,000 years ago. God had laid obligations on the people and in so far as they had failed to fulfill them, they felt themselves in debt to God. Today we would say that "debts" are our sins of omission and commission, the wrongs against God and others that we commit. To confess our sins is to take responsibility for them and not to seek a scapegoat. True confession is a sign of faith maturity.

We ask God for our daily bread and for forgiveness on behalf of ourselves as well as for others. Both petitions go beyond ourselves. To be forgiven by God is to be at peace with God provided we observe the "as" clause in this petition which includes others. Jesus, in His parable of the Unmerciful Servant (Matthew 18:23-25), tells us we have no right to ask for God's forgiveness and have no hope for it if we are unwilling to forgive those who have done us wrong either through omission or commission.

And lead us not into temptation. At first glance, this petition could be mistaken to mean that God leads us into temptation. That is not what Jesus had in mind when he gave us this petition. This petition does mean, however, that temptation and testing are a part of our daily lives. Faith in God does not guarantee the good life and freedom from harm. Our temptations and testings help prepare us for the ultimate temptation in life. Jesus is talking about deliverance from major evil over which we do not have sufficient resources ourselves to defeat. Jesus is talking about the forces of evil that could cause us to forsake our faith and the doing of God's will. Ask your children what would cause them to forsake their faith in God? Would Hitler's gas chambers cause them to lose their faith? What would help them to maintain their faith? What experiences have we had or stories of others that might help our children maintain their faith in adverse times?

But deliver us from evil is the second half of the above petition and clarifies the first half. It prays: "Preserve us, O Lord, from the evil one. We are powerless against the reality of evil unless you come to our aid. Let not our faith in you fail us especially when we are confronted by evil. Help us to recognize the faces of evil found in evil people, evil circumstances, and in evil thoughts." Can our children identify any? How can the kingdoms of this world destroy us physically? Why can they not destroy our souls if God is with us? Jesus' cross, death, and resurrection tell us that evil can destroy us physically and weaken us spiritually, that God is with us and suffers with us, but that eventually God has the last word.

For Thine is the kingdom, the power and the glory for ever. Amen. The Lord's Prayer concludes with a doxology*, with words of praise to God. These words were added perhaps as many as two centuries following Jesus' first utterance of the Lord's Prayer. We can say these words because Jesus revealed to us God's will, God's kingdom, God's power, and God's glory through His life, death, and resurrection. The Lord has power over this world. Yet God restrains the use of that power and requires us to work through our problems. All glory is to be ascribed to God. No evil force can take God's kingdom from God. This doxology liberates us and reaffirms what has already been prayed in the Lord's Prayer.

It is easy for our children to commit the Lord's Prayer to memory. It is more difficult for them and us to live out the meaning of the Lord's Prayer. This prayer sets forth God's terms for true and acceptable prayer. Through this prayer our children and we learn who God is, what our relationship to God should be, whose rule should dominate our lives, what petitions God accepts, and what help we can expect from God.

The Lord's Prayer acknowledges God's supremacy and helps set the model and limits for our petitions, intercessions, and confessions to God. It also gives us the assurance of God's forgiveness. We conclude it with an *amen* which means "and so shall it be."

Our imagination so magnifies the present, because we are continually thinking about it, that we turn eternity into nothing and nothing into eternity.

                                        Blaise Pascal

7

*

How Do Scripture and Devotional Works Help Our Prayer Lives?

Perhaps the most important way to get to know God and ourselves is through the study and discussion of and meditating upon scripture. This practice is an important building block for a realistic understanding and relationship with God. Scripture is one of the ways God communicates with us. It is through scripture your children will learn to communicate with God.

Children are seekers. They are drawn to the biblical story if it is properly presented. The Bible speaks to us in many different voices. It covers a few thousand centuries of people's experiences with God and their interpretations of those experiences. The Bible is a multi-layered collection of various works presented in different literary genres. No one book or no one episode in the Bible can be read in isolation and held to contain all the truths found in the Bible. Each book in the Bible forces us to reconsider and reinterpret every other book in the Bible and our currently held understanding of God.

Early Christians adopted the Old Testament as their scripture because they believed they could not ignore God's revelation as found in the Jewish scriptures. The New Testament was written to preserve people's knowledge and experiences with Jesus. It was written for believers. It contains "faith summaries" reflecting the beliefs of early Christians written long after the death of Jesus. The writings found in the New Testament vary in tone and content depending on the needs of the people and the audience addressed; such as the educated and noneducated; as well as Greek, Jewish, and Roman peoples.

Though many of our ways of experiencing life have changed from biblical times—through technology, knowledge, and the development of new social, political, cultural, and economic institutions—our emotional and spiritual needs have not changed. It is as easy today to identify with Joseph's brothers as it was when his brothers first experienced their jealousy over the preferential treatment Joseph received from their father.

The meaning of scripture is not frozen in the past. Each generation brings its own life experiences to scripture and makes new discoveries. God's Spirit helps us lift the veil covering the meaning of the text. We can help children enter into a conversation with the text and the characters in the story. We can ask them to assume they are one of the characters. What do they think that character is trying to say or achieve? We can ask them to try to envision the story from different perspectives. We can ask them to assume they are the person opposed to God's will and sometimes the person working in accord with God's will. What is happening in the biblical scene? Have them change their roles, their gender, and their age and reenter the scriptural scene. How differently do they experience the story with these changes? How is God's word opening up to them?

Let their imaginations work. Let them pretend they are Joseph the young man, one of his brothers, his father, Potiphar, the chief butler, the chief baker, the Pharaoh. What are their struggles, tensions, loves, hates, desires, and passions? How does each of them suppress these feelings or let them dominate them and why? What happens when they lose control of their feelings? What is good about and what is bad about losing such control?

One or more of the above-listed characters are close to our and your children's inner, hidden personalities, our latent feelings and thoughts, and those of your children. One such latent feeling is the dominant need for approval. We find we need to be affirmed. We come to understand the relationship between God and what we think of ourselves. Could Joseph have survived slavery and imprisonment without a conviction that God loved him? How was Joseph able to forgive his brothers?

When studying scripture in this way, keep all questions open ended and in a "what if?" mode. People then and now have to live life filled with its uncertainties and changing circumstances. To survive, children need to develop critical thinking skills in how to solve the moral dilemmas of life while still staying in a right relationship with God and each other. Listen and allow your children to speak openly in a nonjudgmental, open environment. Set aside your preconceived ideas as to what we think they should be saying. Challenge and listen to the text and to them. In such an environment your children can think beyond their age. Through this method, you will learn as much from them as they will from you about God's word to us.

Children can nourish their spiritual, moral, and intellectual development by studying the word of God. They need not hurry through the Bible. In Sunday school, they can act out different biblical scenes, discuss them by entering into them, and draw their interpretations of them. Most of the Sunday school class is preparation for prayer. Children listen and absorb the message of scripture with its richness in variety and depth of meaning. If the Bible is superficially taught, their prayer will be spiritually impoverished.

It is important to remember that the early church searched the Old Testament to discover the importance and meaning of Jesus. Jesus laid the basis for this search on the road to Emmaus when He said to His disciples:

> "Oh, how foolish you are, and how slow of heart to believe all that the prophets have declared! Was it not necessary that the Messiah should suffer these things and then enter into his glory?" Then beginning with Moses and all the prophets, he interpreted to them the things about himself in all the scriptures.
>
> Luke 24:25-27

In effect Jesus is saying to us that to learn about God we cannot take scripture at face value. Scripture contains many gradations of meanings and interpretations. We only get a fraction of its meaning with each reading. We need to look at the whole and then the parts and then back to the whole.

The prophet Hosea speaks for God when he tells us what the heart of faith and prayer is all about: "For I desire *steadfast love* and not sacrifice, the *knowledge of God*, rather than burnt offerings" (Hosea 6:6).

Prayer is meant to flow from this steadfast love and knowledge of God. Our religious rituals and celebrations are meaningless if we lack love and knowledge. Religious rituals are the outer form of worship. Something must also occur in the inner being. The prophet Amos spoke for God when he said:

> I hate, I despise your feasts, and I take no delight in your solemn assemblies. Even though you offer me your burnt offerings and cereal offerings, I will not accept them, and the peace offerings of your fatted beasts I will not look upon. Take away from me the noise of your songs; to the melody of your harps I will not listen. *But let justice roll down like waters, and righteousness like an ever-flowing stream.*
>
> Amos 5:21-24

Justice and righteousness are the fruits of love, knowledge, and communion with God. Prayer as communion with God should be an integral part of service and mission.

Children are attempting to understand the world around them. They use their keen imaginations. They search stories, myths, fantasies, legends—religious and secular life—in their search for meaning and purpose. That is why they and we are so interested in other people's lives, their stories, especially those of the rich and famous, so that we can find a kernel of truth that will help us explain these riddles of life.

It is also important, therefore, to help them find God through other avenues of exploration in addition to the Bible such as devotional works, edifying literature, and biographies that reveal hope, faith in God, and courage against all odds. Children see with their hearts as well as with their intellect.

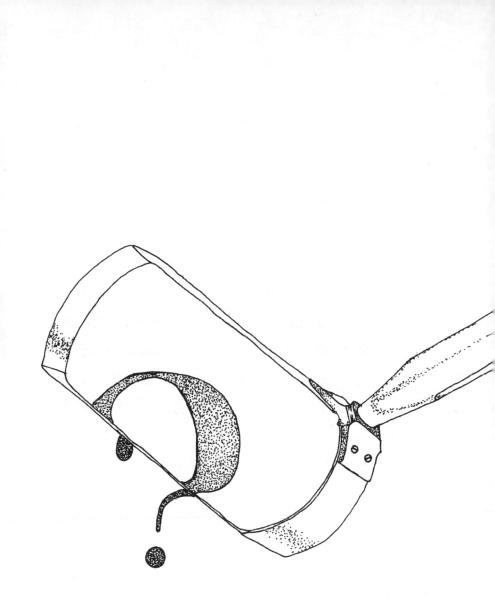

If you find in the Holy Law or the Prophets or the Sages a hard saying which you cannot understand, stand fast in your faith and attribute the fault to your own want of intelligence. Place it in a corner of your heart for future consideration. Do not despise your religion because you are unable to understand one difficult matter.

Moses Maimonides

8

*

Miscellaneous Questions about Prayer

Throughout this book, I have tried to cover in some depth the most important questions we and our children encounter in our prayer lives. What follows will be miscellaneous questions about prayer not covered elsewhere.

1. *I am a Sunday School teacher and I have never taught prayer before. How do I begin?*

The first step is to read the rest of this book with special emphasis on Chapters 6, 7, and 11.

The younger your children, the easier it will be to introduce prayer time into your class rhythm. Young children will follow your lead. If you consider prayer time important, so will they. Have your children participate in getting ready for prayer time. If your class has been working on a project, have them complete it and put it away. Or you may wish your class to have prayer time before any activities begin.

Whenever you think it best to have prayer time, be sure that as many distractions as possible are removed. Create an atmosphere different from regular class time. That means you may want to dim your lights, have each child pick up a carpet square, and sit on them on the floor in a circle. Be natural and at ease with them.

It is important that your children realize that they will be speaking to God and that our minds be on God. Ask them to think about the day's lesson and how we may have experienced similar problems. Let them tell you what they may wish to say to God. And then say something like this: "Let us close our eyes (to reduce distractions) and pray. Dear God, we are glad you want us to get to know you. We are glad that you speak to us through the Bible and told us about the rich man and Lazarus. We now know you want us to share what we have with each other. We_____(let the children fill in the rest). We pray that you will continue to show us how to live. Amen."

For young children, be sure to keep the prayers short and simple. Let each child have an opportunity to say his thoughts. We really cannot and should not monitor their communication with God. If your children seem to be too talkative and just want to hear themselves speak rather than communicating with God and if the time for prayer is about to be over, suggest that everyone now say their private prayers to God in silence. When you think they have had enough time to finish their prayers, say "Amen."

Instead of a written prayer, speak from your heart to God on behalf of your students about the thoughts and concerns expressed in your class discussion.

Young children love a hands-on approach. From time to time change your prayer time format. It might be good to have them set up a little altar made up with a table covering, a cross on a stand, one or two candles. Children can stand around this altar and say their prayers. During Advent, you may wish to bring in some wooden figurines that represent Mary and Joseph as they journey toward Bethlehem. Let your class imagine the people and problems Mary and Joseph may have met on their way. You may even want to repeat a variation of the story from the day's lesson. Let each child put his or her figurine on the altar at the appropriate time in the story. Figurines for parables and other Bible stories can easily be made by people in the parish. Usually some retired people would be thrilled to supply you with a good collection of figurines that can be used interchangeably. Children have great imaginations and they can and do invest figurines with personalities of which we could not even dream.

Older children do not necessarily need or want a hands-on approach. But there needs to be some ritual to follow so that they will have a certain degree of comfort and preparation for prayer. It may be a good idea for them to plan their prayer time. It is good to talk about prayer and the importance of praying. Let them know that reading and discussing the scripture is a part of prayer. It is their part in listening to what God has to say to them.

You may wish to talk about how other people have prayed. Jesus attended worship in the synagogue, read scripture, and prayed there with others. He particularly prayed the Psalms. Jesus also sought seclusion to be alone with God. On the cross, His prayers were brief and urgent with a mixture of anguish and trust.

Muslims pray like Daniel did. Three times a day Daniel turned towards Jerusalem and took time out from his busy schedule to pray. His practice of praying to God endangered his life because he refused to worship and treat Darius I, the conquering ruler of Babylonia, as divine.

Early Christians facing the lions in the Coliseum prayed and sang to God. Their singing of the Gloria Patri unsettled Nero and the spectators. They wondered how these Christians about to die could sing praises to their God. "Glory be to the Father, and to the Son, and to the Holy Spirit, as it was in the beginning, is now, and ever shall be, world without end. Amen."

If you are studying the petitions of the Lord's Prayer, say and sometimes sing it in unison. Sometimes pause after each petition so that everyone can think about the meaning of these petitions and how they apply to their lives.

Have a student or students read part or all of a psalm.

Have a prayer of thanksgiving about the new insight you and your class may have gained from the day's lesson. Ask God for help and courage to live the Christian life.

2. *At what age should I encourage children to pray on their own?*

At home, you as the parent will have to decide when the resistance to prayer reaches a point when prayer time may actually become a hindrance to prayer. It is important that your children willingly carry on an unforced conversation with God. If your child's resistance is great, suggest he continue prayer on his own in the privacy of his room without interfering with the prayer lives of the rest of the family. This approach will allow you to continue praying with your younger children.

But before you allow your older child complete independence, try a change in approach. If you read and discuss something from the Bible as part of your prayer time, encourage your resistant child to be in charge of the discussion. Suggest the child use the techniques for entering the text as given in Chapter 7 under the title "How Do Scripture and Devotional Works Help Our Prayer Lives?" If the resistance continues, let this child pray independently from the rest of the family.

We have to remember that older children need space for spiritual growth. We need to give it to them. All we should do is suggest. We need to show some trust.

In the classroom, do not abandon prayer. Some resistance to prayer may begin as early as the fourth or fifth grade. Encourage your students to look upon the entire class time as preparation time for prayer. Students will not mind a few minutes of prayer provided they are not embarrassed by being asked to pray out loud. Make prayer time a natural, non-threatening part of your class routine. Have some open-ended sentences that you begin and they can finish. Silence is a necessary part of prayer. Do not rush through the silences. Your lesson may have stimulated some thoughts. Students may be thinking and praying silently. If they continue to be silent after a time of silence, you can complete your own open-ended sentence and then say "Amen."

If prayer has not been a part of your Sunday school class time and for those using the *Mustard Seed Series* for the first time in the upper grades, you may want to phase in prayer time more gradually. For instance, it may be well to wait until the Lord's Prayer is discussed in Intermediate Cycle 2. For those in the higher cycles, wait until you discuss obstacles to prayer with Henri Nouwen's *With Open Hands* in Seniors Cycle 1, or with praying the Psalms in Seniors Cycle 2. These three opportunities will stimulate their thinking on prayer.

There should be no interruption in prayer time for those who begin in the early grades and continue with the program throughout all the grade levels.

New children into the Sunday school will have to make the adjustment as they will have to do with everything else.

3. I am starting midyear as a Sunday school teacher. What should I do?

Speak to other teachers and find out what they do. It is possible that their styles have not worked. Do not be discouraged. Speak to your Director of Christian Education or your Church School Coordinator. Read and study this book. Then decide which approach will be best for you and your class based on your leadership style and your perception of your students' learning styles and needs. You cannot nor should not be a clone of your predecessor. Children need to be exposed to several different teaching, learning, and leadership styles as well as ways of praying.

4. Praying with children is new to our Sunday school. How do we coordinate our efforts so as not to confuse them?

The best approach would be to have several meetings with teachers, minister, parents, and Director of Christian Education present. All of them will become for a short time in their lives the spiritual directors of your children. Perhaps a couple of chapters of this book could be read and discussed at each meeting. Go slowly. Object to what bothers you. Be open to God's Spirit. Be concerned about your children's spiritual growth and all that hinders it.

After deciding on some general outline for proceeding for the different aged children, begin implementing the program. There needs to be honest feedback and continual analysis and revision of your approach by all involved, including your children. Some will prefer one approach over another, that is all right; flexibility and variety are important. Methods will and should change as we and our children change and grow in the faith. No one approach is "right." In fact, a mixture of formal, fixed prayer coupled with extemporaneous prayer may go a long way in meeting the needs of your children in communal prayer. No grade can be given for our prayer lives. What is most important is our opening ourselves to God's presence, God's activity in our lives and in our history, and communing naturally with God.

Patience at home and in the Sunday school are necessary. Do not look for something to happen. A disciplined approach is necessary, however. Breakthroughs and special moments with God will come in the most unusual ways. I can remember my days as a school volunteer. I was an English teacher and decided to give a couple of mornings a week in helping children. One boy I was tutoring was dyslexic. He was bright but could not put a written sentence together. He spent all of his time trying to cover up his problem. He had to learn to accept me and my efforts. He had to realize that I accepted him as he was and not as he thought he ought to be. It took several months to work through these interpersonal dynamics. Then one day, he dropped his posturing and began to learn what I could teach him. A few short weeks later, he was writing sentences and spelling most of his words correctly. Looking back on this experience, I was frustrated with him and was tempted to ask to work with another student who could benefit from my expertise. What a mistake I would have made had I given up on him. God is patient with us. We need to be ever so patient with our children.

At home, do allow and encourage private prayer time and spontaneous prayers for our children. Encourage them to read their Bibles (or children's Bibles) and to think about what God might be saying to them. Or provide them with good devotional literature with interests and concerns on their learning level that can help act as a springboard to prayer. Other times, let them pray their joys and disappointments out loud without making them feel self conscious.

It is important to have some coordination within the Sunday school and between the Sunday school and home on how to approach prayer. Teachers may want to concentrate on developing a particular category of prayer that goes along with their lessons. Or, during prayer time, they may wish to teach their children over a period of time these different categories of prayer. Parents may have different needs and thoughts. It is important to remember that all adults involved be deliberate and that they take their time. In the church and in order to maintain continuity between teachers and parents, make tape recordings or videotapes of your various group meetings and subsequent follow-up sessions. Have these recordings available for new people who come into your church so that they may know the route everyone is taking.

5. *What image of God would be best for me to use with children?*

A lot will depend on the age, knowledge, and maturity of your children. The question of images should be an important part of the discussion between the home and the church.

I have suggested in Chapter 9 that Jesus is God's clearest revelation of what God is all about. Jesus is God incarnate. However, very young children will not understand Jesus' significance. Help them view Jesus as their friend rather than in terms of His divine mission. For those using the *Mustard Seed Series*, the concept of redemption is introduced to children with C. S. Lewis' *The Lion, the Witch, and the Wardrobe* in Intermediate Cycle 2. Through this story form, they will begin to understand the spiritual reality and meaning of the death and resurrection of Jesus Christ. Then other images such as the Lamb of God, Suffering Servant, and bread of life can be added.

Before this grade level, another image the children will most be able to understand is God as Creator and Protector. You may well disagree with these suggestions. But before you come to any decision, be sure to read Chapter 9—Who is God to Whom We Pray?

6. I am a Sunday school teacher. What do I do with children in my class who come from homes that do not pray?

I think it important that children participate at least in the first fifteen or twenty minutes of worship. In that time they will have experienced some prayer, music, and hymns. Many churches have a children's story before dismissing them from the worship service. Children who have this opportunity during worship are introduced to intergenerational prayer and worship. They notice other people's reverence and awe and wish to be a part of it. They should look forward to this time in church.

Sometimes, however, young children are kept too long in church. They have to sit through lengthy prayers, music in foreign languages or by concert soloists, neither of which is suitable to children. Music should speak to their minds and hearts and stir their souls.

Children may never hear about prayer outside the walls of the church. If you have developed a prayer life, talk about it, how it was when you first started, problems along the way, and how it is doing now. If prayer has become easier now than before, explain why. By praying together and talking about it, we may awaken prayer in them.

Listen to their concerns and questions. Admit what you know and what you do not know. Tell them that we are all learning together. We are all on a spiritual journey in life. Each one of us is at a different place in the journey. We can learn from those who travel the road with us. Each day and especially each Sunday we all can learn a little more about prayer.

7. What do I do with children who act up during prayer time?

Very often stress causes inappropriate behavior in young people. Some young people may giggle uncontrollably while others may cry. I can remember an incident when I took a ninth-grade confirmation class on a retreat. This class had never participated in the Lord's Supper. We had discussed the meaning of it, and they were nervous about being admitted to the Lord's Supper. A couple of boys could not stop giggling. They were not being disrespectful. They just did not have control over their emotions at that particular time. I recognized the cause of their behavior and ignored it while continuing preparing everyone for reception of the eucharist.

A few days later a mother apologized for her son's behavior. I had not mentioned it to her. Her son must have been so embarrassed by his behavior that he wanted his mother to smooth things over for him with me. The next time I saw him, I told him I understood and not to worry about his behavior. Next time he takes communion, he will not be as nervous.

If a young person is deliberately disrespectful, speak to him after class. Find out what his problem is and try to resolve it then and there. If the problem is serious, refer it to your Director of Christian Education or minister.

8. I am a parent who does not know how to pray. How can I help my children?

You are not alone. Many, many people do not know how to pray or are uncomfortable praying. The best advice I can give you is to study this book thoroughly and adopt what you can from it. If there is coordination between the church and home, you may learn from each other. Maybe your minister may be able to help you or recommend some books or biblical passages suited for your needs. You could read, discuss, and meditate upon the Bible and devotional literature. This process will stimulate clearer insights into what God is all about. You may even find the process suggested in this book for the various age levels helpful in your own spiritual journey.

Prayer will grow naturally as you consciously stay on your spiritual journey. Do not be anxious about your prayer life. Do not let others make you feel inadequate. Only God and you are privy to your relationship. Let that relationship develop naturally as it would with a friend.

9. How do I respond to questions like "My parents don't pray, why should I?"

Whatever you do, be sympathetic to the parents' position. A teacher's response to this question could be that they may not know how to pray or that there may be some obstacle to prayer in their lives. Say: "Your parents may not understand what prayer is all about and that is why they send you here. Perhaps what you learn in Sunday school you can share with your parents." Ask him if his parents would like to *borrow* this book to learn more about prayer. Tell them we are a faith community committed to helping each other and that we are connected to each other through Jesus Christ. Part of our living out of our faith is to be in communion with God through prayer. And we would like his parents to join us.

10. I believe in God, but somehow I do not feel God's presence. What's wrong?

All people experience at one time or another spiritual dryness. During these times, do not give up praying. Instead pray the classic models of prayer. They are rich in their brevity and simplicity. In time, they will enable you to reestablish your communion with God.

11. Times are bad. Why shouldn't I be anxious about tomorrow?

We all have had or are living through difficult times. But as Jesus said: "Do not worry about tomorrow, for tomorrow will bring worries of its own. Today's trouble is enough for today" (Matthew 6:34). We have to live one day at a time. We have to take care of our daily needs. We are to pray to God for our daily bread. If we worry about tomorrow, we fail to live today fully. And the nervous energy we put into worrying about today and tomorrow may deplete us of our energy and ability to function. Of course, these statements do not mean that we do nothing. We have to work. Jesus is not implying that tomorrow will be better than today. What they mean is that we are not to be *anxious*, that worry accomplishes nothing and blocks our ability to trust in God.

12. Is it all right to ask for God's help on a test, to win a race, to find a job, to win a war?

There is no problem in asking for God's help. But we also have to keep in mind that part of our task in life is to do the very best we can and to keep our wishes in accord with God's (see Chapter 6 on the Lord's Prayer and the petition entitled "Thy kingdom come, thy will be done.") For instance, the son of a Seventh Day Adventist who excelled in track told Robert Coles, a researcher and author of *The Spiritual Life of Children*, how he prayed before a meet. He said:

I asked God, please, to let me do the best I could. I didn't ask [God] to make me the winner, no sir. I used to want to win the races, but my daddy and our minister said it's not the winning, it's the running with God's blessing, that's what counts. Just because you think of God, and you pray—[God's] not the One who will take sides and push you so you can beat out others.[2]

Elaborating further on the answer to this question, Bill Huebsch in his book entitled *A New Look at Prayer* told of his desire to win a high school football game. On the morning of the football game, he went to chapel to cover all his bases for success. When he arrived, he found the opposing team there. He wrote:

I knelt down, realizing I was in the heart of the enemy, aware that I was the only one from the other team who was present. The senior captain was leading a prayer.

But he wasn't praying for victory! He was praying for charity, for fairness, and for an honest game. He asked God for the inner strength to be a humble winner—or a graceful loser—and he prayed that, in the final analysis, our lives together in our community would be made more joyful, that our brotherhood would grow stronger from this contest on the playing field.

He took the wind out of my sails!

I learned something that day that I've never forgotten. God is love, and the one who lives in love, lives in God and God lives in him or her. God's power affects our inner lives, our hearts, and *we* affect the world. God's intervention, if we can call it that, is an intervention of love in our inner lives. We need but open our minds and hearts to it.[3]

13. Does God answer our petitions?

Yes, but we might not always know, understand, recognize, or accept God's answer.

Our expectations of God might be unrealistic. Even Christ questioned God's intent in His final hours. He questioned why

God did not come to His aid. Jesus uttered His feelings of desolation and abandonment by God in those wrenching words which come from Psalm 22: "My God, my God, why have you forsaken me?" On the cross God revealed God's method for dealing with the world. It is not one of glory. Jesus showed us humility, weakness, and vulnerability as God's answer to our petitions. Most of the time God refrains from using God's power.

We learn from Jesus that there are some situations we have to endure. We learn that God in Jesus participates in our suffering and sorrows. Personal tragedy and sorrow usually cause us to despair and become disoriented. We do not know what to do. We are in unfamiliar territory, alone, and frightened. We learn from Jesus' crucifixion and resurrection that God's ways are not our ways. They are mysteries.

14. Christian discipleship is often the way of the cross. Should I encourage children to live as Christians?

Yes, if you want your children to have life and have it more abundantly. Do help them to understand the meaning of discipleship, its costs, and what it is to be a Christian. The choice is theirs. Our existence comes from and depends on God. Jesus asked us to renounce self-centeredness, to deny self, and to follow Him when He said:

> If any want to become my followers, let them deny themselves and take up their cross and follow me. For those who want to save their life will lose it, and those who lose their life for my sake, and for the sake of the gospel, will save it. For what will it profit them to gain the whole world and forfeit their life?
>
> Mark 8:34-36

15. But Jesus told us to ask for whatever we need and He will provide. Is not the above answer a contradiction to what Jesus said?

No, it is not. Jesus asked us to align ourselves with Him and with His kingdom and to forsake our kingdoms. We might even say that this alignment is a precondition for our petitions. A Christian life should not center around personal property and personal power. Jesus said:

> If you abide in me, and my words abide in you, ask what you will, and it shall be done for you. By this my Father is glorified, that you bear much fruit, and so prove to be my disciples.
>
> John 15:7-8

Our petitions to God all need to be viewed in the light of our identifying with Jesus. *Everything is to be done for the glory of God and not for our benefit or glory.* Answers to our petitions may not be the answers we expect or want even though Jesus says many times throughout the gospels:

> Ask, and it will be given you; seek, and you will find; knock, and it will be opened to you. For everyone who asks receives, and he who seeks finds, and to him who knocks it will be opened.
>
> Matthew 7:7-8

Jesus is saying that *He will give us the strength and courage for the Christian mission and our Christian journey* and that eventually we will be rewarded. But this reward may not necessarily be material or physical. The reward will be spiritual.

16. Well, what is the Christian mission?

The Christian mission is to live out our lives in faith in God, our Creator, Redeemer, and Sustainer, in conforming our will to God's will, and to carrying forward Jesus' work.

17. What then does it mean to be in conformity with God's will?

Refer to what was said under the petitions of "Thy kingdom come, Thy will be done, on earth as it is in heaven" under the Lord's Prayer, Chapter 6.

The result of all prayer should be communion with God and conformity to God's will*. Instead, most of our prayers are an attempt to conform God's will to ours. We try to convince God our way is the right way.

18. How does prayer help give us direction for and unity to our lives?

A scribe once approached and asked Jesus which commandment comes first. Jesus answered:

> The first is, "Hear, O Israel; the Lord our God, the Lord is one; and you shall love the Lord your God with all your heart, and with all your soul, and with all your mind, and with all your strength." The second is this, "You shall love your neighbor as yourself." There is no other commandment greater than these.
>
> Mark 12:29-31

If we prayerfully live out this Great Love Commandment, it will transform our inner lives and will be expressed externally as well. We know from our personal friendships and loves how special people and their ideas and spiritual qualities affect us. Through our intense relationship with them, we become sensitive to everything they think or do. As with these people, persistent fellowship with God will change the quality and tone of our lives. We become God's agents and instruments in this world. Our attitudes and motivations will reflect this internalization of the Great Love Commandment. Our prayer lives help us in serving God and our neighbors. They are not for our private advantage.

19. Will God forgive my sins?

Yes, God will forgive those who truly repent.

Many of us today think we live good lives. And according to our secular society, we do. We are not murderers or robbers and many of our deeds are honorable. Yet our hearts may be filled with rancor, deceit, and covetousness. We may not hunger and thirst after righteousness for the oppressed.

Some of us may be weighed down by guilt. When we beg

God for forgiveness, we put pride aside. The psalmist expressed our need for forgiveness when he said:

> Have mercy on me, O God, according to thy steadfast love;
>   according to thy abundant mercy blot out my transgressions.
> Wash me thoroughly from my iniquity, and cleanse me from
>   my sin...
> Create in me a clean heart, O God, and put a new and right
>   spirit within me.
> Do not cast me away from your presence, and do not take your
>   holy spirit from me.
> Restore to me the joy of your salvation, and sustain in me a
>   willing spirit.
>
> Psalm 51:1-2, 10-12

In our gratefulness for being forgiven, we put our lives at God's disposal. We are grateful for a second chance. We will try to be God's agent and instrument in this world.

20. My child is handicapped. I have prayed and prayed that he may overcome his handicap, but he has not. Why has God not answered my prayer?

God has allowed all of us to be born differently from each other. Some of us are born female and some male, yet we each share masculine and feminine characteristics. We are born into different economic levels, different nationalities and races. Our skin, hair, and eye coloring, height, weight, health, and intelligence are determined by the genetic make up of our ancestors. Our lives are influenced by these circumstances, limitations, and possibilities.

To ask God to change our physical makeup is to ask God to violate God's natural laws for our advantage. I do not believe we should ask God to set aside the laws of nature, our handicaps, sex, race, and the like. We can ask God to help us live with them. Our limitations teach us something about ourselves. We learn we are finite and mortal, that we are not in charge of the universe. We learn we can overcome or manage with some handicaps and limitations and not others. We pray for God's help to make us better, stronger, and more understanding people. We use our gifts and time to do the best we can.

Years ago I was a Director of Christian Education. In the Sunday school there was a beautiful girl, Tasha, who was deaf. She had to work double time to keep up with her peers. Rarely did she flag in her zest for life. Her mother refused to put her into a school for the deaf. She was mainstreamed educationally and had to endure the cruelty of her peers as they would laugh at the strange sounds that represented her attempts at speech. Her self-image was low. And her parents were going through a bitter divorce which she could not understand in her silent world.

When she was in fourth grade, we were preparing a Christmas pageant based on *The Littlest Angel.* She asked me if I thought the director, a very talented and caring person, would let her be in the pageant. This director had the true Christmas spirit. She would not exclude any of God's children. She wrote an extra part for Tasha. The girl standing next to her helped her as well.

The director decided to write an announcement for the birth of Jesus and wondered if Tasha would be able to speak it. I saw no reason why she could not; she was working very hard on her lines with her speech therapist. We knew she would rise to the occasion.

The day of the pageant arrived. The hall was crowded with families and friends. Tasha was superb. Those who did not know her never guessed that she was deaf. Those of us who did know wept. Tasha's friends, family, and speech therapist praised her and gave her roses in recognition of her performance. For once in her life she was publicly affirmed. And she has never been the same since.

From that day on, Tasha began to accept herself as she was and to use the gifts God had given her. She started taking responsibility for her life. No longer would she let her deafness and feelings of rejection defeat her.

In high school she played basketball, volleyball, and was a star on the track team. Now she is in a first-ranked college earning A's.

I am sure that Tasha and her mother prayed for Tasha's deafness to be removed so that she could be like other young people. I am sure God heard their prayers. And God answered them in an unexpected way. Instead of granting her her hearing, God granted her a healthy, positive self-image, and that has made all the difference.

God does answer our prayers but often in unexpected ways.

21. What other ways does God answer our petitions?

Sometimes God says "no" to our petitions. Often our petitions are denied us because if answered they would cause us or someone else harm. A gun is not something we would give to a small boy. Sometimes our petitions are at cross purposes to God's will or other people's needs. Our petitions may be denied us so that a higher and better blessing may come to us or someone else. An unknown Confederate soldier said it well when he wrote:

He asked for strength that he might achieve;
    he was made weak that he might obey.
He asked for health that he might do greater things;
    he was given infirmity that he might do better things.
He asked for riches that he might be happy;
    he was given poverty that he might be wise.
He asked for power that he might have the praise of men:
    he was given weakness that he might feel the need of God.
He asked for all things that he might enjoy life:
    he was given life that he might enjoy all things.
He has received nothing that he asked for,
    [he has received] all that he hoped for.
His prayer is answered.

Additionally, prayers of intercession may be denied because the person we wish to help does not want help or is not ready to take responsibility for his or her life. For instance, if an alcoholic or someone with an eating disorder refuses to seek help, there is nothing more God can do because God does not want to deny that person his freedom. Similarly, Jesus was unable to convert or change much of the world.

Answers to some petitions may be deferred. Genuine prayer that meets the criteria set forth by Jesus in the Lord's Prayer is eventually answered. It may be deferred to teach a spiritual discipline. For instance, Hannah, the wife of Elkanah in 1 Samuel 1, was unable to conceive a child despite her fervent prayers. Then she made a vow that if she were to have a son she would consecrate that son to God's service. When Samuel was born to her and after he was weaned, she took him to the temple at Shiloh and put him in the care and tutelage of Eli the priest. Samuel was dedicated to the Lord. W. E. Biederwolf suggested:

> If Hannah's prayer for a son had been answered at the time she set for herself, the nation might never have known the mighty man of God it found in Samuel. Hannah wanted only a son, but God wanted more. He wanted a prophet, a ruler, and a savior for His people. Some one has said that in this stance "God had to get a woman before He could get a man." This woman He got in Hannah precisely by delaying the answer to her prayer, for out of the discipline of those weeks and months and years there came a woman with a vision like God's, with tempered soul and gentle spirit and seasoned will, prepared to be the kind of a mother for the kind of a man God knew the nation needed.[4]

What we learn from Hannah is that if an immediate answer to our prayers is obtained too easily, we may not necessarily value the gift. We may take the gift for granted.

Some petitions asked will not be answered. They may be frivolous. For instance, we may pray for spring to arrive in the winter or for winter to occur during the summer.

Other prayers may be deferred until we work out within ourselves whether or not that which we desire is truly the will of God. If it is the will of God, we should persist and be patient. If it is not, we should change our prayer.

God gives us what we need and not necessarily what we want. James Hastings, the author of *The Christian Doctrine of Prayer*, said:

> We pray for physical good, and God answers with spiritual life. We pray to be freed from the burden, and God answers with patience and strength to endure. We pray to be spared the conflict, and God gives us courage to fight the good fight of faith. The great end of religious effort is a developed soul, a soul with a deep sense of God, a soul in which faith, courage, and resolution are at their highest.[5]

22. Will God send me signs to indicate God's answer to my petition?

Sometimes God will send us signs, but we are not to expect them. Jesus responded to the Pharisees' request for signs with this answer:

> An evil and adulterous generation asks for a sign, but no sign will be given to it except the sign of the prophet Jonah. For just as Jonah was three days and three nights in the belly of the sea monster, so for three days and three nights the Son of Man will be in the heart of the earth. The people of Nineveh will rise up at the judgment with this generation and condemn it, because they repented at the proclamation of Jonah, and see, something greater than Jonah is here!
>
> Matthew 12:39a-41

Jesus expects us to live and walk by faith in Him. It was not difficult for Jonah to convert the gentiles of Nineveh. All Jonah had to do was proclaim God's word to them. Jesus is greater than Jonah. His life, death, and resurrection are all the sign the people need.

23. *How do I explain to my children about the evil and the suffering that exist in the world?*

The Book of Job and Jesus' cross help give an answer to this troubling phenomenon. Perhaps God allows evil and suffering to exist to instruct us. English author Samuel Johnson made the point that our lives are short and that God can rectify over eternity the apparently unmerited suffering that we witness and experience now.

In the Book of Job, Job and his friends argued over why he was suffering so many misfortunes. Job's friends accused him of doing some evil thing. They believed that God acts in a contractual way. They believed if anything goes wrong in our lives, it is our fault. They told Job to confess his sins. Then God would hear his prayers and would respond favorably to him. Job, however, claimed his innocence and would not confess something for which he was not responsible.

Job did not follow their suggestions. Job was a rebel. Job continued to pray to God but would not submit to what was not true. Job's friends suggested that Job placate God by telling God that God was right and that he, Job, was wrong. What Job's friends did not realize is that we can question and challenge God about the way life is working or not working out for us.

Job needed to be honest with God. He believed there was no warrant for the treatment he was receiving. And God agreed with Job's position in Job 1. Job was innocent. But Job did not have any right to condemn God for his lot in life. In Job's encounter with God, God asked Job: "Will you condemn me that you may be justified?"

Out of the whirlwind, Job learned that God is in charge of the universe, that moral and cosmic order are not the same, that the way God governs the universe is beyond human comprehension. Certainly God does not govern it by a contractual arrangement with human beings as Job's friends believed. Job learned that God is not answerable to us. God never gave an explanation for the cause of Job's suffering. It is enough to be allowed a relationship with God. It is enough to meet and know God. God informs Job that complete knowledge of God and God's ways will not be granted him and by analogy us.

Job's story sheds some light on the cross. We may have to live a sacrificial life and suffer evil, and die a cruel death as Jesus did. We may be asked to be faithful during periods of what we imagine to be complete abandonment and forsakenness by God. Jesus' cross also tells us that God suffers with us. Jesus is God among us. Jesus was as vulnerable as we are. His resurrection assures us that God will rescue us from perpetual evil. We will have to pray for God's help in keeping the faith. (See the petition "Lead us not into temptation" in the Lord's Prayer, Chapter 6.)

24. Why should we sing praises and thanksgivings to God?

Prayer is more than petition. Prayer is praise of God. The first part of the Lord's Prayer states who God is and our relationship through Jesus to God. The doxology or the ending of the Lord's Prayer affirms God's glory, power, and self restraint. Nothing, no one, and no evil force can defeat God. God is gracious to us, loves us, forgives us of our sins, and is present to us. We are a privileged people to know and have access to God. This access is symbolized by the tearing of the Temple veil at Jesus' death. We are allowed to draw near to God as a child would to a parent, simply, honestly, and openly with no hidden agenda except to love and to express our love to God.

God helps us get through the dark night of our soul. God's presence tells us that we will never be left destitute. God welcomes and encourages us to carry on Jesus' work.

We thank God for God's self-giving love. God's love opposes and stands in contrast to all the meanness of life that can darken our lives.

God is the source of all life. Jesus called Himself the living water. As Jesus said to the Samaritan woman in the gospel of John:

Everyone who drinks of this water [at Jacob's well] will be thirsty again, but those who drink of the water that I will give them will never be thirsty. The water that I will give will become in them a spring of water gushing up to eternal life.

John 4:13b-14

Those of us who have observed springs cannot tell from where the spring comes. But we see water bubbling up through the earth watering, nourishing, and giving abundant life to all that is within its flow. Without water life cannot exist. And by analogy real life does not exist for those who are separated from God, the source of all life. And for these reasons we praise and thank God.

25. *A child once asked his teacher if God spoke to him as God did to Mr. G.? What was his response and what should my response be in a similar situation?*

This teacher was taken aback by the earnestness of the child's question. Silence fell over the classroom. Evidently all the other children wanted to know the answer, too. The teacher answered that God does not speak to him directly but that God speaks to him through what is written in the Bible, through other people, through the beauty he finds in a sunrise and a sunset, the vastness of the ocean, the power in a waterfall, and so forth. God does not speak to him directly in a voice. He believed God does not need to use God's voice to speak to us.

This teacher reported that a wave of relief swept over his class. He surmised that Mr. G. used God's voice as a way of establishing himself with that class. It turned out that class members had a terrible sense of guilt and unworthiness because God did not speak to them personally. Their teacher's response removed this burden from them. (Refer to the section Prophetic and Biblical Revelations in Chapter 9 for more information.)

26. *Why do some people say that service is a necessary part of prayer?*

If we pray for God to help us and our neighbor without our willingness to cooperate with God, our prayer is false. We all have certain survival needs. We do not know when our survival will depend on someone else. Jesus relates our service to Judgment Day when He said:

> "Come, you that are blessed by God, inherit the kingdom prepared for you from the foundation of the world; for I was hungry and you gave me food, I was thirsty and you gave me something to drink, I was a stranger and you welcomed me, I was naked and you gave me clothing, I was sick and you took care of me, I was in prison and you visited me." Then the righteous will answer him, "Lord, when was it that we saw you hungry and gave you food, or thirsty and gave you something to drink? And when was it that we saw you a stranger and welcomed you, or naked and gave you clothing? And when was it that we saw you sick or in prison and visited you?" And the king will answer them, "Truly I tell you just as you did it to one of the least of these who are members of my family, you did it to me."
>
> Matthew 25:34a-40

Christian service identifies with the joys, sorrows, and needs of other. We are to do for others what is within our ability yet resist the tyranny of overwork.

All our deeds are to be done for the glory of God, in love, and in humility. Our attitude is important. Are we really ready to be used by God? What follows is an adaptation of a person's plea to God to do God's work. "E.H." stands for Eager Heart.

E.H.: "Lord, give me loftier views of Christ."
God: "Yes, I will; but first you must have deeper and more humbling views of yourself."
E.H: "Lord, use me to do great things for you."
God: "Yes, but are you completely willing to be only the tool, and not the hand that moves it?"

E.H.: "Lord, I would like to be filled with your Holy Spirit and power; will you make me a brilliant lamp, giving clean and steady light?"

God: "Yes, but I must first empty you of all your own oil, and so make room for that fulness of the Spirit to get in."[6]

Christian service may be our volunteer efforts in easing people's misery by providing and helping in soup kitchens, free medical care for the needy, mission schools, providing temporary and permanent shelters for the displaced and the homeless, and introducing legislative action to assist the marginalized and oppressed within our society.

Young people can do Christian service as simple as visiting shut-ins, being a Big Brother or Big Sister to a child in need of a friend, raising money or contributing a portion of their allowance or earnings to worthwhile causes to working or rehabilitating homes of the needy. All this service should be given joyfully and in Jesus' name.

27. What will happen if I do not pray?

You will not come to know God. Friendships take time to develop and cultivate. If you do not pray, your spiritual life will be diminished.

28. Will going to church be sufficient communion with God?

Church is an enormous aid in communing with God. But we need to remember that public worship is the outer form of worship. Something needs to occur in the inner being, too.

29. How can I fight off destructive temptations and become a better person?

Resisting the small temptations in life helps prepare us for the big ones. Temptations are our inner struggles and conflicts.

Prayer reminds us of God's will and of God's vision for us. Temptations are similar to the lure of alcohol a reformed alcoholic senses. The inner struggle and battlefield are great. Only God and our support group can give us the help we need to survive. Remember, you are not alone.

Prayer helps us control our emotions which are dominated by our right brain. Prayer helps us align our will with God's will and to defeat or block out unwholesome anxieties and desires. Prayer helps us achieve a proper tension between our right brain and our thinking, rational left-brain activity. Our left brain tells us to align ourselves with and petition to Jesus for help in fighting off temptations. (See Chapter 12.)

30. My soul is troubled. How can God help me?

Jesus opened His Galilean ministry with a composite reading of Isaiah 61:1-2 and 58:6 with these spiritually revolutionary words. He said:

> The Spirit of the Lord is upon me, because he has anointed me to bring good news to the poor. He has sent me to proclaim release to the captives and recovery of sight to the blind, to let the oppressed go free, to proclaim the year of the Lord's favor.
>
> Luke 4:18-19

Jesus is issuing a program of amnesty and liberation. He is introducing a healing ministry that will free us and open the doors of our dark, airless prisons. Jesus is asking us to let go and release all that holds us in bondage.

If we ask, God will forgive us and restore our spiritual sight as we turn from the darkness to God's light. If we come to Jesus and ask Him, He will release us from our negative emotions. If we ask and cooperate with Jesus, positive emotions can take over and bring us into a relationship with God. Ask and we will receive God's spiritual gifts. Our salvation is in the Lord.

My atheism, like that of Spinoza, is true piety towards the universe and denies only gods fashioned by men in their own image, to be servants of their human interests.

George Santayana
Soliloquies in England

*

It is essential that God be conceived as the deepest power in the Universe; and second, that God be conceived under the form of a mental personality. God's personality is to be regarded, like any other personality, as something lying outside my own and other than me, and whose existence I simply come upon and find.

William James

9

*

Who Is God
to Whom We Pray?

Implications of Socialization

Doctrines and creeds have attempted to describe and explain God and God's actions. It seems to me they fall short in explaining God, especially for children's understanding. Part of the problem seems to be that we cannot adequately describe the Infinite and that which is indescribable. By necessity we use symbolic language and comparisons when talking about God. Symbols and comparisons are only pointers and a close approximation of a greater, deeper reality.

Many of the images used in the Bible and in ritual prayer have lost their power and meaning. We need to rethink and redefine for our children the words and images we use for God. It is important we save enduring past images of God with the understanding that *no one image is sufficient. Each image reveals only a limited attribute about God and does not reveal all there is to know about God.*

We can tell our children that God loved us so much that God came to us in a form we are able to understand. God came as the baby Jesus who grew up just like we grow up. We learn the most about God through God's prophets and the life and death of Jesus.

Research studies on how children develop their understanding of God and how that understanding influences their lives are detailed in Robert Coles' *The Spiritual Life of Children.*

He showed how children filter information and events and make determinations about God and the world based on this filtering process. The home environment helps shape children's psychological images and understanding of God. He found that children project onto God their understanding of their parents and environment. For instance, if a child has a loving parent, then God will be perceived as a loving parent. But if a child has an abusive parent, that child often has a distorted perception of God.

Robert Coles' studies covered over thirty years of in-depth research and a very large sample of children from different regions and social-economic levels around the United States and the world. Coles believes that most children do not have a physical image of God *unless* it is given them by a parent, teacher, or through some artistic representation. If children do have a physical image of God, that image follows along racial and ethnic lines. Usually God has no gender. Jewish and Muslim children are forbidden to have an image of God.

Robert Coles gives an example on how we can unwittingly stifle our children's religious curiosity and growth. He tells of a bright nine-year-old boy who lived in a working-class white neighborhood of Boston. Coles asked him (Tommy) to draw a picture of God. Tommy asked Coles if he should draw the picture of Jesus found in his church's stained glass windows. Coles told Tommy that he would be delighted to see whatever images of God Tommy might wish to draw.

Tommy then wondered out loud what God looks like. He asked Coles: "Do you think He looks like us?"

"I don't know."

Tommy said: "I don't think He does. He might look real different...like something that doesn't even exist here."

Tommy continued:

> In Sunday school...[our teacher] showed us a picture of Jesus and asked us to copy it. She told us to be very, very careful, because it's God we're copying. My friend asked if God and Jesus look the same. The...[teacher] told us they *are* the same! I wanted to ask some more questions, but I could see she wasn't liking us asking any. She told us to "get down to business," and we sure did, right away! She carried this [blackboard] pointer around with her, and if she didn't like what you said or the way you questioned her, she'd slam it down on your desk, and you knew what she was telling you: next time it'll be your hide![7]

It is our job as significant adults in the lives of our children to create an open, trusting, non-judgmental environment where children can feel free to wonder, to express their doubts, and to ask questions. No question is dumb or inappropriate, especially as it relates to belief, faith, and developing understanding. We set the tone for discussions and our children's learning.

Children ask deep, penetrating questions about God, creation, disasters, oppression, belief, and faith. These questions are a necessary part of their developing spiritual selves, curiosity, and prayer lives. Many of their questions are our unanswered questions. We should not let our lack of knowledge close the door on their inquisitive minds. They need to know our present thoughts. They need to know that we, too, are interested in having clearer understandings along the lines of their questions and that we will try to explore more deeply their questions with them, with other adults, with the clergy, and through continuous study of scripture. Humility can go a long way. We are not authorities on everything. *Our knowledge about God is limited purposely by God.*

Coles told us of his conversation with a ten-year-old Hopi girl who was described by her white teachers as not being particularly bright. He wrote:

That same girl, months after the conversation about the thundercloud, talked of a Hopi struggle with the Navahos which was then taking place, a contest for land: "They [the Navahos] want the land, and we believe it has been here for us, and it would miss us."

I [Coles] asked how the land could "miss" a group of people.

"Oh," she replied, "the land can feel the difference."

I asked her, "How?"

"The Navahos want to dig and they want to build. The land will be cut up....When it is quiet, really quiet here, we'll all be with God—the Navahos and us, and the Anglos. The land will be with God, and not with us."

Did she have any idea when that time would come? No, she most certainly did not. But she was "pretty sure" of this: "Our people are here to wait until the time comes that no one hurts the land; then we will be told we've done our job, and we can leave."[8]

Over the next few years, Coles came to appreciate "this girl whose heart beat to Hopi rhythms and whose soul lay open to an entire landscape."[9] *Coles and I believe we do not have a sufficient understanding of children's moral and faith development.* This Hopi girl illustrates how studies with their questions and selections of answer a, b, c, or d often reenforce the bias of researchers that fit people into neat categories.

Robert Coles' method encouraged the children with whom he worked to lead the way. He wrote:

Prolonged encounters with children are the essence of the clinical work I learned to do in hospitals and of the work I do in the homes and schools I visit. Each child becomes an authority, and all the meetings become occasions for a teacher—the child—to offer, gradually, a lesson. My job is to listen, of course, and to record, to look (at the pictures done), and to try to make sense of what I have heard and seen. My job, also, is to put in enough time to enable a child like the Hopi girl to have her say—to reveal a side of herself not easily tapped even by good schoolteachers.[10]

Children's social and physical environment shape their beliefs. It is important for us to be aware of the positive and negative influence we may have on them and their spiritual development. Our children are our trusts for a limited time. They are a gift from God whom we are called to mold and shape into righteous, God-loving human beings.

Our emotional baggage affects our and our children's lives. Authority figures in children's lives can take on God-like or demon-like possibilities. For instance, children are trying to understand the world around them. They may project onto authority figures their wants and fears. For many children, there is a small jump between the authority figures in their lives and their image of God. As authority figures, we may unwittingly stir their imaginations and fears with either tyrannical or God-loving images.

We all live less than ideal lives. We are not perfect. But with God's help, we can all try to live better lives and be better people no matter what our emotional, spiritual, social and economic circumstances may be by constraining our destructive behavior. Our improved personality will ultimately help our children. It is never too late to turn to God and to seek God's help.

Prophetic and Biblical Revelations

Many positive biblical understandings of God come from the Old Testament. Old Testament prophets knew God as *will and personality*. They believed God has a vision for us, loves us, and wishes to be in relationship with us. Old Testament prophets believed God is not bound to time, space, or gender and does not need eyes and ears to hear and see. Yet God possesses personality traits such as thinking, willing, feeling, loving, and grieving. The prophets believed we are able to come to God with our joys, our sorrows, our praises, and our complaints. We know God hears us, is present to us, and will comfort and help us. God participates in our lives even though we cannot see God.

In the book of Exodus, when God asked Moses to return to Egypt, Moses asked for God's name. God purposely veiled God's essence with this answer: "I AM WHO I AM" (Exodus 3:14).

Many years later and after many miraculous experiences with God, Moses gives his people his parting wisdom about God on the Plains of Moab. Moses disclosed the oneness and unity of God when he said:

> Hear, O Israel: The Lord is our God, the Lord alone. You shall love the Lord your God with all your heart, and with all your soul, and with all your might. Keep these words that I am commanding you today in your heart. Recite them to your children and talk about them when you are at home and when you are away, when you lie down and when you rise.
>
> Deuteronomy 6:4-7

Many centuries later, when questions arose as to whom Jesus was, Jesus repeated Moses' understanding about God's unity and oneness and added: "You shall love your neighbor as yourself" (Mark 12:29-31). The oneness of God, our expected love and devotion to God, and love of neighbor is known as God's Great Love Commandment. This commandment sums up Jewish faith and life and became the guiding principle of Christian faith and life.

The Jewish people were and are strict monotheists. They believe in only one God. In the Old Testament, Jewish people believed God became known to them through God's Spirit.

In Genesis 1:2, it is the Spirit of God that is moving over the face of the waters. God and God's Spirit are at the beginning of creation. Old Testament people believed God and God's Spirit to be one.

During the time of the Jewish exile in Babylonia, Jews began to wonder whether Yahweh was just a national god, an inferior god, or the supreme God above all other gods. Babylonians were saying that their god was superior to Yahweh because he helped them conquer the Jewish people. Because of Jewish bewilderment, disorientation, and despair, Isaiah II reestablished

in the people's minds God's supremacy. Isaiah spoke for God
when he said:

> Before me no god was formed, nor shall there be any after me.
> I, I am the Lord, and besides me there is no savior....I am the
> Lord, your Holy One, the Creator of Israel, your King.
>
> Isaiah 43:10b-11, 15

Some priestly writers during the Exile squelched this notion
of Yahweh's inferiority by writing Genesis 1. In this chapter,
God is the creator of the universe, of the sun and the moon, of
the stars in the sky, the birds in the air, the animals of the
earth, the fish of the sea, and lastly, human beings. Genesis 1 is
a rebuttal to anyone who thinks their god or gods, be they
wooden images or modern technology, are supreme and in
charge of the universe.

During the Babylonian exile, Isaiah spoke for God when he
said:

> To whom will you liken me and make me equal, and compare
> me, as though we were alike? Those who lavish gold from the
> purse, and weigh out silver in the scales—they hire a gold-
> smith, who makes it into a god; then they fall down and wor-
> ship! They lift it upon their shoulders, they carry it, they set it in
> its place, and it stands there; it cannot move from its place. If
> one cries to it, it does not answer or save anyone from trou-
> ble....Remember this and consider...I am God, and there is no
> one like me...I will fulfill my intention....I have spoken, and I
> will bring it to pass.
>
> Isaiah 46:5-11

The Old and New Testament tell us that God is Spirit. There
is no accurate or realistic picture we or our children can form
of God because none of us have seen God or been given an image of God. God dwells in no particular place.

Throughout the ages, God has spoken to us through the
prophets. Prophets are very special people called by God and
filled with God's spirit. They have acted as the spiritual and
moral conscience of their country. They have felt an irresisti-

ble, divine compulsion to speak what God has revealed to them.

An important point to make here for our children's benefit is the distinction between true and false prophets. In Old Testament times, kings hired court prophets. Often these prophets in order to gain favor with the king disregarded what God's will* was and what their consciences told them. Prophets who remained outside the official circle generally were more truthful and were often mocked by the court prophets. Kings knew that what the non-court prophets said was generally true. They chose, however, not to heed what non-court prophets had to say.

In every age there have always been a lot of false prophets that say they speak for God. Cult leaders and many TV evangelists have spoken as though they were God's prophets. Some of them paint either a rosy future or pictures of doom and gloom for their followers. Our young people, who are still developing their spiritual lives, may become confused. They need some valid means of determining who are the true and false prophets of today.

James Carse, Chairman of Religion at New York University, wrote:

> The history of attempts to speak for God is notorious. One could reasonably argue that acting as though one had the authority of the divine is itself the very source of evil. We very seriously misunderstand the nature of evil if we think that persons act out of true malice. Virtually all evil is done in the interest of the good.[11]

Our minds can play dreadful tricks on us. We cannot represent to each other with absolute certainty that God speaks to us and that what we think God says to us is the absolute truth and represents divine authority. "Generally, if not always, it is quite impossible to distinguish between the voice of God and the voice of our own best conscience and ideals."[12] God may be trying to speak to us:

according to our capacity to understand. If our windows are soiled, the sun's rays are hindered; but that fact is no denial of the truth that whatever light does come through our windows comes from the sun.[13]

Therefore, only the exceptional prophet can speak for God and then only in a limited way. The prophet is limited by his humanity. Knowledge of God and God's will is filtered through such constraints as time, place, personality, environment, and society. James Carse gave a very good reason why God restricts us. He wrote:

If I speak to you with the authority of God, I violate the limitations of our humanity in two ways: I regard myself as something considerably more than human, and I regard you as something considerably less than human.[14]

A few other criteria for helping our young people determine who are the true and false prophets of today are:

1. Do not always believe those who tell you what you want to hear. They may not be honest with themselves or with you.

2. The majority opinion may not always be the best opinion because it is easier to go along with the majority than to stand alone for your convictions.

3. How trustworthy have the "prophet's" forecasts been in the past?

4. Do the "prophets" speak for God or for their own or someone else's self interest?

5. How close to the doing of God's will as given to us in scripture are these "prophets'" pronouncements?

Some early and negative Old Testament images of God need to be understood as part of the evolving theological process of people's developing understanding and interpretation of God and God's actions. For instance, God is not a God of war as suggested in the Book of Joshua. The writers of this book, however, did interpret the collapse of Jericho as God's victory. In later Old Testament writings and from Jesus' ministry, we learn that this early perception of God is incorrect.

Jesus—God's Clearest Revelation of God

God did not have much success with God's prophets. God's next move to bring people into a closer relationship with God was to come physically into our midst as the Christ. In Luke 1:35, it was God's Spirit and power that came upon Mary. She conceived and bore Emmanuel, God with us.

Jesus was like any other human being. We often give children the notion that Jesus was not human, that Jesus was solely God. We need to emphasize Jesus' humanity. His physical and mental growth pattern were similar to ours. He was vulnerable to rejection, temptation, love, suffering, hope, despair, and death.

Jesus developed a vision of how life ought to be lived which was also in part defined by his physical and mental human limitations, thought forms, and the political, social, and religious dynamics of His day. In His three temptations in the desert, Jesus made a decision not to seek control over people's lives by feeding them, by wooing them with spectacle, or by selling His soul to evil forces in exchange for worldly power and the opportunity to do good. Jesus decided to win people's hearts through love and not force and through whatever sacrifices were necessary to bring them closer to God.

The Jewish authorities during Jesus' life and after His death and resurrections reacted violently to Jesus' claim of a special and equal status with God. To the monotheistic Jews these claims were blasphemous and heretical. The charges leveled against the early and modern church are that we are polytheists, that we believe in more than one God, that God, Jesus, and the Holy Spirit are separate deities.

These challenges to Christianity caused Jesus' followers to abandon old thought forms. They had to rethink how Jesus, God, and the Holy Spirit can be one yet different.

The early church spent several centuries trying to work through a doctrine of the Trinity. God's Spirit and God were viewed as one and the same both by the Jewish believer and the Christian. But who was Jesus?

Controversies raged in numerous specifically convened councils on the oneness of God revealed to us in God the Creator (Father), God the Redeemer (Son), and God the Sustainer (Holy Spirit).

These councils are historically and theologically important because they show us some of the controversies with which the early church had to deal and the social construction of the theology behind the doctrine of the Trinity.

Most Christians believe in the oneness of God as revealed in the Old and New Testament. Bernhard Lohse in *A Short History of Christian Doctrine* outlined Augustine's understanding of the Trinity that many believers accept. He wrote:

> There is no activity...in which only the Father, or only the Son, or only the Holy Spirit is involved....Augustine conceives the unity of the Trinity so stringently that he asserts that not only the Father, but also the Son and the Holy Spirit, were actively involved in the incarnation of the Son....the three persons of the Trinity always work in concert.[15]

There is a unity of operation in the Trinity. To put this doctrine on a more practical and mundane level for our understanding, we might draw an analogy to the different roles we assume in life. For instance, I am a wife, a mother, and a minister. Certain individuals know me better in one role than in another. Yet I am the same person and I am involved in all three roles. Because I am one person, each of my roles somehow interpenetrates or influences my other roles. Yet no one role is dominant over the other roles.

Can We Answer the Question— ### Who is God to Whom We Pray?

Yes and No. As the foregoing part of this chapter indicates, metaphors, symbolic, and analogical language may point to a greater reality than what they represent, but they are incomplete and do not describe God.

Our prayer lives reflect our understanding of God. By necessity, they are limited by our human, mental, physical, spiritual, and emotional limitations. God cannot be contained by and known completely through doctrines, creeds, prophetic revelations, Jesus' revelations, death, and empty tomb. If we try fully to define God, we are bound to fail.

God gives us only a partial knowledge and understanding of God through Jesus, the prophets, other believers, and historical events. They are all parts of a limitless whole. As God said to Moses, what has been revealed to us should be sufficient. "I AM WHO I AM."

It is important to emphasize that God is not like a human being and has no gender. No one knows what God looks like. The use of masculine pronouns followed past grammatical rules and men's desire to discriminate against women by equating their gender superiority with God's superiority. Today, when referring to God, more inclusive language is used.

When we are open to God's presence, we learn about, see, hear, and experience the unseen and unheard. We come to know God's actions in the world. God encourages us and our children to have a loving and prayerful relationship with God. Prayer is often wordless. Prayer is the awareness of being in God's presence. Prayer is our response to God in faith and love. Prayer is our sharing of eternal life with God.

There must be rough, cold weather,
    And winds and rains so wild;
Not all good things together
    Come to us here, my child.

. . . .

So when some dear joy loses
    Its beauteous summer glow,
Think how the roots of roses
    Are kept alive in the snow.

Alice Cary
November

10

*

What Can Happen on the Journey of Parenthood?

A new relationship begins between a couple when they decide to have children. They are making a commitment to love and care for their children. Their decision binds them to each other and to their children in a unique, non-repeatable relationship.

Because of our children, our life styles, spiritual journey, and freedom take on new meaning. They force us to make decisions differently than if we had no children. We find we cannot run in all directions at one time without tearing ourselves and our relationships apart. Our commitments and journey limit us and in other ways they open up unforeseen possibilities which add excitement and newness to our lives.

Often our relationship with God has its peaks and its valleys. Some of the valleys are difficult to understand. They may be an obstacle in our efforts to guide our children. Some of these experiences will be discussed in the remainder of this chapter.

A Cry of Absence

Some of us might feel ill-equipped to make a spiritual journey with our children because we have not felt God's presence in our lives. Our intellect tells us there is a God, but our heart may remain unmoved. We may even practice a form of philosophic prayer (see Chapter 12) to guide our moral lives until God becomes known to us. Some children may experience this same absence of God. We need to let children and those of us who experience this absence know that it is all right. These valleys may be part of the journey.

Many, many people fall into this category and stand at some distance from the Christian community. They are not hypocrites and will not feign the joy other Christians experience. Unfortunately, the Christian community judges them harshly and fails to accept them and where they are on their spiritual journey. That does not mean that God has abandoned them. There is no special status for those inside the church over those outside the church. We do not know God's thoughts. Instead of our adverse judgment, church people should be warm and accepting of them. They should help them in whatever way they can on their spiritual journey. And maybe, God's plan for them may be different from what church people would prescribe.

We all know very good people who are seeking to have faith and trust in God. They may have even tried to master all the techniques of spiritual directors to no avail. The Bible is full of people's dismay over God's absence. The psalmist cries out:

Why, O God, do you stand far off?
Why do you hide yourself in times of trouble?

Psalm 10:1

And

How long, O God? Will you forget me forever?
How long will you hide your face from me?

Psalm 13:1

And

Create in me a clean heart, O God,
  and put a new and right spirit within me.
Do not cast me away from your presence,
  and do not take your holy spirit from me.

Psalm 51:10-11

During the Babylonian exile when the Jewish people felt forsaken by God, the prophet Isaiah said: "Truly, you are a God who hides himself" (Isaiah 45:15).

Later on, God replied:

For a brief moment I abandoned you, but with great compassion I will gather you. In overflowing wrath for a moment I hid my face from you, but with everlasting love I will have compassion on you.

Isaiah 54:7-8

Even Jesus experienced the absence of His total trinitarian Godhead on the cross when He cried out these forlorn words: "My God, my God, why have you abandoned me?" (Matthew 27:46).

I truly believe that God does not wish us to forsake our desire for God's presence. For whatever reason God may be absent from us today, God's presence will be restored to us. Isaiah encourages us to continue in our search. He said:

Ho, everyone who thirsts, come to the waters;
  and you that have no money, come, buy and eat!
Come, buy wine and milk without money and without price....
Seek the Lord while he may be found,
Call upon him while he is near;
  let the wicked forsake their way,
  and the unrighteous their thoughts; let them return to the Lord,

that he may have mercy on them, and to our God, for he will
abundantly pardon.
For my thoughts are not your thoughts, nor are your ways my
ways, says the Lord.
For as the heavens are higher than the earth, so are my ways
higher than your ways
and my thoughts than your thoughts.

Isaiah 55:1, 6-9

We all are in process—all on the journey of life. Part of that
journey is spiritual whether we acknowledge it or not. Some of
us are exiles in a strange land while others of us have the privilege of being in God's presence. But that privilege of being in
God's presence carries a greater responsibility to do God's
will*.

Children are one of God's way of leading and bringing us
into God's presence. Look upon their lives, their need for
Christian nurturing, and their spiritual development through
prayer as a mutual opportunity for a closer, clearer relationship with God.

Trust

If we are to guide our children's spiritual journey effectively, we need to remember that it takes time and their experience
with us to establish a trusting relationship. The older our children become, the more distrustful they are of those adults and
friends who have violated their confidences and inner space. If
children distrust us, they will try to avoid us or will not speak
their thoughts even though they desperately need our help.
Love, patience, honesty, openness, sincerity, sensitivity, and
participation in their lives are essential in establishing a loving
and trusting relationship with them.

Trusting in God, we will journey with them into the spiritual world while remaining in the physical world. We will look
for the deeper meanings of life. We will ask ourselves the
meaning of events we are experiencing and how to interpret
them. What is God trying to say to us? What inner vision is

God giving us? Perhaps only time will unravel the mystery of any given moment.

Presence

If we have a relational problem with our children, part of that problem may be that we are not always present to them. As busy parents with active minds, we may become bored with their activities, chatter, and exploration of the world. We may become exasperated with their desire to hear the same story over and over again. We want adult conversations and adult company.

For whatever reason, our bodies may be present to our children but we may be absent to them because our minds are not engaged with what they are saying or doing. This phenomenon happens not only with our children but also with our spouses when we read the newspaper, a book, or watch an exciting television program. We are inattentive to the others in our presence.

Unfortunately, this same process has happened to many of us in our relationship with God. God has been and is always present to us. We may not acknowledge or feel God's presence because we may be too absorbed in other things. Then when we look for God, we may not know how to find God.

If we are interested in teaching children how to pray, we, too, have to learn how to pray. We, too, have to find our way into God's presence so that true prayer can begin.

For many of us, there are obstacles to our participating in a prayer life. It is as though we have come up against a huge, lengthy wall which blocks our access to God. We know there is a door but cannot find it.

I will not go into the many different ways of knowing. Philosophers debate empiricism versus rationalism, faith versus reason, the limits of knowledge, and so forth. Philosophical inquiry works with suppositional frameworks that try to prove whatever argument is presented. Faith and God cannot be reduced to these frameworks. Faith goes beyond the straitjacket

of reason and challenges us with uncertainty, risk, and commitment. As Paul said:

> Faith is the assurance of things hoped for, the conviction of
> things not seen. For by it the men of old received divine ap-
> proval. By faith we understand that the world was created by
> the word of God, so that what is seen was made out of things
> that are not visible.
>
> Hebrews 11:1-3

An artist friend once wrote to me:

> I have been thinking about prayer and my creative pursuits a
> lot lately. I have trained my eye to see very clearly and have
> disciplined my hand to record what my eye is seeing. Prayer,
> for me, mirrors the *mind/eye/hand* relationship. Through disci-
> pline and practice, the relationship comes very naturally, al-
> most without thinking. It just happens. When inspiration
> strikes and the discipline is innate, then the creative result is
> very satisfying and fulfilling. Inspiration comes frequently es-
> pecially when I am open to it. But without practicing the neces-
> sary skills, I usually find the final result falls short of my vision
> and the process is frustrating instead of a flowing pleasure.[16]

Like my friend, we and our children need to learn to be at-
tentive to God in prayer, to learn to see with our inner vision
and hear with our inner hearing how God is present and active
in our lives.

Crisis Situations

Part of our spiritual journey may include trauma such as
when a child runs away or a loved one is on his deathbed.
We may be struggling with an addiction. We may feel rejection by society or we may be lonely. Women may think their
biological clock is running out. Older men may feel threat-
ened by younger men. Or we may be suffocating with guilt.
Whatever our problem, we are living and trying to survive
the crises of life.

Children live in crisis situations, too. We may think their problems are inconsequential, but their problems are just as great to them as are our problems to us. For instance, they may have lost a parent, a grandparent, or someone else who is special to them. Every time they see another child have that special relationship with a family member that is denied to them, despair may set in. Rejection and insensitive treatment by peers and adults can be devastating.

In desperation and feelings of helplessness, many of us turn to God. Somehow we know God hears us and understands. The relief we get from God may not be exactly what we want, but it is sufficient.

For instance, a good friend's son could not stand the constraints of conventional society during the turbulent sixties. His solution to his problem was to leave home at age sixteen with no forwarding address and no communication with his family for fear he would be forced to return home and to their society. For six months, my friend and her husband did not know whether their son was alive or dead. The heartbreak and uncertainty was more than she could bear. Finally, she prayed that God would let her know at least where he was. Shortly thereafter, a state policeman from a distant state called her to say they had picked up her son. He still did not want to return home; but by that time, she and her husband accepted his desire to live apart from them. All they wanted to know was that he was alive and well; other issues could be worked out somehow.

The ultimate crisis situation is the deathbed. Many of us fear death, but Christians believe there is life after death, that their perishable bodies are replaced by an imperishable body in the spiritual world. Some people die without making their peace with God; other people are healed spiritually even while they are dying. Perhaps the most disquieting situation for us is when a child's life hangs in the balance between life and death. Some of us may be like the father in Goethe's *The Erl-King*.

O who rides by night thro' the woodland so wild?
It is the fond father embracing his child;
And close the boy nestles within his loved arm,
To hold himself fast, and to keep himself warm.

"O father, see yonder! see yonder!" he says;
"My boy, upon what dost thou fearfully gaze?"
"O 'tis the Erl-King with his crown and his shroud."
"No, my son, it is but a dark wreath of the cloud."

The Erl-King Speaks
"O come and go with me, thou loveliest child;
By many a gay sport shall thy time be beguiled;
My mother keeps for thee full many a fair toy,
And many a fine flower shall she pluck for my boy."

"O father, my father, and did you not hear
The Erl-King whisper so low in my ear?"
"Be still, my heart's darling—my child, be at ease:
It was but the wild blast as it sung thro' the trees."

Erl-King
"O wilt thou go with me, thou loveliest boy?
My daughter shall tend thee with care and with joy;
She shall bear thee so lightly thro' wet and thro' wild,
And press thee, and kiss thee, and sing to my child."

"O father, my father, and saw you not plain
The Erl-King's pale daughter glide past thro' the rain?"
"O yes, my loved treasure, I knew it full soon;
It was the grey willow that danced to the moon."

Erl-King
"O come and go with me, no longer delay,
Or else, silly child, I will drag thee away."
"O father! O father! now, now, keep your hold,
The Erl-King has seized me—his grasp is so cold!"

Sore trembled the father, he spurr'd thro' the wild,
Clasping close to his bosom his shuddering child;
He reaches his dwelling in doubt and in dread,
But clasp'd to his bosom, the infant was dead.

The accidental death of a loved one challenges our faith. Since it occurs quickly, we do not even have time for a prayer of intercession. But what about a child or adult who languishes with an incurable disease? We try everything medical science can do for them. When known cures do not work, we try one experimental treatment after another. We earnestly pray that they may be spared. Their quality of life is gone. Yet we cry foul when they die.

Why did God not answer our prayers? We ask that question and so will our children. How do we answer? We might suggest that death is sometimes a gift especially when pain and misery have been lifted. New life begins with God. Life after death does not belong to a grey nether world of an Erl-King.

Death is a natural part of life. Often our genetic coding determines our life span. From the beginning, God has placed limits on our mortality. We are not God and cannot live forever in our present form. I look and feel differently today than I did ten years ago. Aging and dying are an inevitable part of life.

Elisabeth Kubler-Ross wrote a letter in answer to the questions of a nine-year-old boy with cancer. He asked: "What is life?...What is death?...And why do young children have to die?"[17] Her letter known as the "Dougy Letter" relates our life cycle and its duration to that found in plant life. We are like the dandelion seeds that are blown either onto lush lawns or into the cracks in an impoverished neighborhood. No matter where we are God loves us. Then she compares school to our life process where we learn about ourselves and others, where we learn honesty, love, and giving, where we pass the tests of life, graduate, and return home to God. Our lives are like plants. Some live for a shorter and some for a longer period of time. What is important for the dying child to know is that he can let go of life, be

free of fears and worries—free as a very beautiful butterfly, returning home to God which is a place where we are never alone—where we continue to grow and to sing and dance, where we are with those we loved...and where we are surrounded with more love than you can ever imagine.[18]

The dying usually are ready to leave this life. It is the living who make it difficult for the dying to die. The living often make the dying feel guilty that they are leaving them. It may be unfair and selfish of us to deny the dying a new life.

Some of us may turn away from God because of tragic events. Others of us will turn to God in our hurt and brokenness. We seek God's help in healing the great void and woundedness we are experiencing. And in our very brokenness, we will find God. As Psalm 23 so clearly states, we all must pass through the valley with the shadow of death in it. We cannot walk around it or be carried over it. We must go through it. What God will do for us in our extremity, if we let God, is to be present to us to guide and comfort us.

Psalm 22 which Jesus had in mind when he said from the cross: "My God, my God, why have you forsaken me?", suggests first, that God did not spare Jesus and by extension will not spare us and second, that we may even have to endure feelings of abandonment during times of trial.

But Jesus' resurrection tells us that after we journey through this dark valley, we will enter into new light, a new life, and a new beginning. New life comes out of our experience of the darkness.

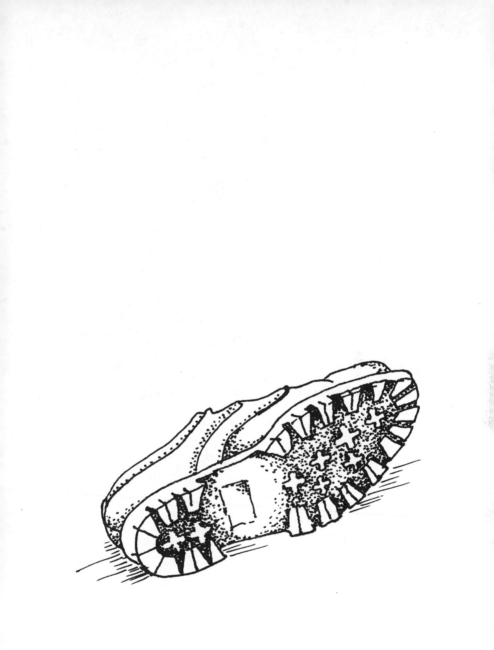

It is good for us that we sometimes have sorrows and adversities, for they often make a man lay to heart that he is only a stranger and sojourner, and may not put his trust in any worldly thing.

Thomas à Kempis

11

✳

Necessary Steps and Stops along the Way

Just as an artist or an Olympic star needs patience, practice, training, and a willingness to go beyond the ordinary to achieve his final goal, so must we not expect too much of ourselves or our children. Prayer is not a chore but an experience with God that grows as our experience with God grows. Let us then not hurry the process. Let us and our children take one step at a time.

What follows will be *possible* steps and stopping places for us in guiding our children's prayer lives from infants to teenagers.

Many comments that I will make about an earlier developmental stage may still apply to a later stage. Very often we will have to let our children lead us in our efforts to help them. Let their needs, concerns, personalities, and learning styles dominate how they engage in communion with God. No one method, no one viewpoint will ever work with all children. They are so different and bring their different world environments and understandings to their spiritual lives. For instance, we can all look at the same picture or hear the same story. The objective reality of the picture or story remains the same, but our children and we will have our own unique interpretation of what we see and hear.

First Steps and Stops

When babies actively explore their environment and slowly begin to realize that they and their environment are not the same, the process of self differentiation begins. They react and respond to whatever stimulus affects their physical senses and emotions. If their environment is hostile and/or loveless, they will withdraw into themselves. If their growing steps are met with love, acceptance, and encouragement, they will continue to take more new steps and grow emotionally, spiritually, intellectually, and physically.

Parents and surrogate parents are babies' closest approximation and understanding of God. Our treatment of them, as Robert Coles discovered, will give them their initial understanding of God.

So at this stage the most important step in developing our children's spiritual lives is to give them our love, our attention, and our time. We need to be present to them and earn their trust in us. They need to feel emotionally and physically secure even when there are the inevitable tensions in home life.

No two adults live together in perfect harmony. Disagreements that occur in front of our children or behind closed doors may threaten their sense of security. Our children need to learn that healthy disagreements and resolutions of them are an important part of negotiating life lived in community. They are acceptable behavior. But violent behavior and loud shouting in an effort to achieve control over another person is sick, unacceptable behavior. Most children will mimic our behavior.

When we are cuddling or feeding our babies and youngsters, we can be saying or singing short prayers. Whatever we do, use good grammar and keep sentences short and simple. Talk to them about God, about how God loves them, about God coming as a baby into our world, how baby Jesus was tiny like they, how baby Jesus grew a little bit each day, how He loved other babies, how He loved the flowers that grow in the garden and in the fields, how He loved the birds that fly in the air, how He loved the ants that crawl on the ground, the rain and the sun that make it possible for things to grow, and so on.

Children's initial education is through their senses with the help of their motor muscles and nerves. They need to see, touch, hear, taste, smell, and put into their mouths or caress most everything in their environment. Encourage this education of their senses. It should be a lifelong process. It is right-brain activity and an important part of learning about life. Left-brain or rational activity begins about age two with the development of language. (See Chapter 12—Mystical Prayer.)

As our children's world opens up to them, explore it with them. Try to see their world through their eyes. Marvel with them at the wonders of this world. Tell them how God made this world and how we are supposed to use it and protect it. Examine with them the beauty of a flower, a butterfly, a stone, or a seashell. Then thank God for giving us such treasures.

Help our children identify with the growing Jesus. It would be well for children to think of Jesus in human terms of growing, eating, sleeping, getting bruised, and learning about God and the universe.

Children see things we cannot see. When they are young, they are closer to the ground and have not trained their minds as most adults have to shut out observation and appreciation of certain parts of the universe. Children, if they have not been anesthetized by television, spend much of their time in wonder. They see their world as one big place for exploring, to roam through without any pressure of time, to jump from one interesting observation and thing to another. Their growing muscles keep their bodies on the move. They are in perpetual motion. Their minds are creating universes that exist partly in this world and partly in another world.

When we read to our children an illustrated children's book or Bible story, they are not so concerned about what we read as they are by the illustrations they can see. They see things in the illustrations that we would never observe. They will put their fingers on the pictures. If the book has a little fuzzy, they will touch it. Vicariously, children will jump into the illustrations in order to explore that world on the page before them. Give them all the time in the world to wonder, wander, and use their imaginations in this way.

When we read to children what is printed in illustrated children's books, we are in effect teaching them how to associate what they are hearing with what they are seeing and feeling. Therefore, it is necessary to have good illustrated children's books on prayer and Bible stories. If these books try to portray what God may look like, stay clear of them because nobody knows whether God has a body, form, or gender. And we do not want them to have to unlearn the bad theology some illustrations teach them. If children's books have drawings of Jesus, be sure that no one image or picture dominates because none of us knows what Jesus looked like. What we do know is that He was a man and was truly human as well as divine. Different male images are acceptable so long as no one particular static image dominates.

Let books on God and on prayer be a natural part of their daily routine. These books are teaching them about God. They are planting moral values and a moral standard for the way they make critical life decisions.

Illustrated children's stories that are morally inspiring also help our children grow up into loving and unselfish Christians.

An Important Stop—Prayer Times

Some families, especially those with young children, find it best to have set prayer times as a part of the rhythm of their lives.

In Europe during the Middle Ages and (even today in some

rural European communities), when church bells rang at regular intervals, people stopped their work to pray. The artist Jean François Millet had an interesting painting entitled "The Angelus" in which two workers in dirty work clothes stopped their work to pray during the tolling of bells. Millet illustrated that life, work, and prayer are not compartmentalized but are all connected. Our lives are more hectic and run on a more unpredictable schedule than lives lived in earlier times. Expectations run high. Modern time-saving conveniences encourage us to accomplish more than those living in a previous age. The pace of our modern lives, however, is no excuse for ignoring God's presence and for not engaging in conversation with God.

One good way to begin to pray with children is by noting what a great gift God is giving us in allowing us to talk to God. We can say to our children: "I know you are now old enough to begin talking with God. We will talk to God in the morning when we get up, during the day when we feel like it or when something special happens, before meals, and before going to bed. I know God wants to hear from us often." Make no apology for past neglect of prayer in their lives. If we are positive about prayer, they will willingly follow our lead and will look upon these prayer times as an opportunity to have ours and God's attention. If we have more than one child, alternate between family prayer and one-on-one prayer.

Dinner time is an especially good time to ask God to be our guest and to be present with us. It is a time to thank God for the earth and the bountiful fruit it yields for our benefit. Too often we think we alone are responsible for the food on our tables. And in a way we are. If we do not work for money, we will not have money to buy food to put on our tables. But if it were not for God's good earth and the minds we have been given to cultivate the earth and to make a living, we would be unable to survive. For these reasons, it is only right to express our thanksgiving to God.

Many families like to join hands when saying grace before meals. This gesture connects us and emphasizes our unity while maintaining our individuality. Other families make the sign of the cross before and after grace is said. Still others have a different family member say grace before specific meals. It is important that children not be embarrassed in their childish efforts at saying grace. Let what they say be the natural outflowing of their thanksgiving and love for God. Parents can help set the pattern of what to say during grace. In fact, many families have a memorized prayer. But we can all do better than that. We need to get away from unthinking, rote prayers and use our imaginations and ability to speak to God. We can speak as freely and naturally as we do about everything else in life. We can speak to God as a close friend. It is not so much how we say our thanksgivings but the genuineness of our thanks that counts. (See Chapter 13 for examples.)

Bedtime and evening prayer should not be omitted because of a television program. This time is a special time for relaxation and intimacy with our children. It is a time to address their immediate needs. It is a time to examine the events of the day, a time to talk about upcoming events, and a time to ask and examine questions about life that may be on their minds.

Children love a story to be part of their evening ritual with you. They love to hear about people who knew God and what happened to them. Simplified Bible stories and other people's stories about where they believe God was active in their lives should be a part of our children's evening ritual. Children will live these stories vicariously. Allow time for discussing any questions they may have about the stories read to them. There is no need to moralize about these stories. A good story will make the point without any need for further comment.

When discussion time is over, suggest that we be quiet before God before we speak to God. During this silence, encourage our children to turn their full attention to God. There is mystery in this encounter. We cannot speak for our children. We cannot put words into their mouths. Children need and want to speak for themselves. They may wish to discuss with God their struggle with the dominant themes or concepts presented in their bedtime stories as well as those events that have shaped their day.

Children may wish to say their prayers out loud or silently. Children do not need ready-made prayers. They have rich imaginations. Let them use them. Let them speak naturally and from the heart to God.

Morning prayer should also be encouraged. Those of us who leave the house early in the morning, if at all possible, allow an extra five, unhurried minutes with our children for prayer time. If we think prayer time is an important time out of our busy schedule, so will our children. As they grow older, they can pray on their own. When we open our day to God, we have a clearer sense of direction and purpose in life and are able to live as Christ's disciples in our daily lives.

In the morning, we can thank God for protecting us through the night. Morning prayer can be made up of short, individual prayers and reference to God's special action as revealed in the preceding evening's discussion and Bible story. And we can thank God for the beautiful sunny day or rainy day we are about to have and ask that God be with us to comfort us, to guide us, and to show us the wonders of God's creation.

A Few Miles Down the Road

Children in the age group of two to five are very exciting to watch grow and blossom. In part of their world, reality and fantasy blur. Their world is egocentric where everything revolves around them. Everything they see and do relates to themselves.

They have little or no *internal* moral reasoning. They determine the rightness or wrongness of a particular act by whether they are punished or rewarded. For instance, if Joey is hitting his little sister over the head with a toy, he does not internally recognize his behavior as being wrong until we tell him that he must not do it. Usually, he will ask us why he can't hit his sister. Then we will have to explain that boys and girls do not hit little brothers and sisters, that they need our protection, that we love him but not his hitting his sister. It is important to maintain the child's self-esteem. If this line of reasoning does not work with Joey and if he persists in hitting his sister, we may have to spank him gently and send through his sensory nerves the painful message to his brain that he will be punished if he hits his little sister. Or we may prefer to make him sit quietly for five minutes for misbehaving.

Likewise, if Joey helps his little sister by pulling her wagon for her or by sharing his toys with her, we can compliment him and help reenforce this behavior and build his self-esteem by giving him a hug. The message that he is to be good to his little sister is learned verbally and physically.

As parents, we may be chagrined at our children's behavior and wonder what type of children we have. Since children at this age tend to live and play as autonomous little human beings, the rightness or wrongness of their actions is spontaneous without any premeditated thinking on their part. We need to remind ourselves that our children's self-centered behavior is perfectly normal and is part of their survival instinct.

When it comes to praying with children, it is best not to encourage them to petition God for things other than the necessities of life. Young children are unable to understand and differentiate what petitions are in accordance with God's will and what petitions serve self-interest.

Young children have no need to praise or flatter anyone. In fact, they do not understand what the word praise means. Flattery and praise are not part of their survival tactics. Therefore, teaching children prayers of praise before they can appreciate why is unnatural.

Young children, however, are capable of adoration. They love life and can easily express their love of God to God. It is easy and natural for them to say, "God, I love you." "Baby Jesus, I love you." "Jesus, you are my best friend."

There is a story I heard a few years ago where a young mother was doing her Christmas shopping with her four-year-old child. As the frantic mother was rushing from one store to another, the child stopped to gaze at a crèche scene in a store window. When the mother realized that her child was missing, she had to retrace her steps to find her. As the mother approached the child, the child exclaimed with joy: "Look, Mommy, there is baby Jesus! See baby Jesus!" The frantic mother did not appreciate the wonder of this moment. She did not realize that at this very moment she could bond with her child and see with her child's eyes. It would have been an educable moment for them both. Instead, the mother pulled her child away from this crèche scene which so captivated her child with these words: "Come on. We do not have time for that now." I wondered what Christmas gift did the child need most?

The Christmas and Christian story is not a still life replica in a store window. It is not something that happened only in the past. It is our story today as well. We own it. We need to take time to be a part of it and to share it with our children so that it can be part of their spiritual journey.

Space, Reverence, and Position

Churches are buildings set aside for the worship of God. They stand on holy ground. They have an aura of the sacred about them. Unfortunately, today criminal activity dictates that many churches keep their doors locked. Except for worship times and choir rehearsals, people are denied access to this sacred space, a place where they could go, be quiet, feel secure in God's presence, and communicate their innermost thoughts to God.

One Sunday after worship service, a young family with a little girl entered the church. She was almost three years old and was put into the nursery before worship. She wanted to see where her parents prayed. She stood in the center aisle and just gazed in wonder at all she saw. Then she slowly walked all over the church, went up in the altar area, examined the organ, and kept looking up at the high, vaulted ceiling. At that moment, I am sure God was with her, and she was aware of God's presence.

Children need to understand the importance and the privilege of being in God's holy place. We should not let our children treat sacred space like play space. Sacred space needs to be approached and entered into with awe and respect. Children should be kept in the church's nursery until they are capable of some self control and reverence. Misbehaved children gain nothing from being in church. They disturb not only their parents but other worshippers as well. It is important, however, that they learn how to act in church by other people's example.

There is something special about space that has been dedicated specifically for worship. In our homes and in our Sunday school rooms, it is important to create a worshipful space and an atmosphere conducive for prayer. Help our children find a prayer place. Prayer space might be a corner of a child's room or at the side of a child's bed, or a special rock out of doors or on or under a tree.

In order to avoid the temptation of ostentatious piety, Jesus suggested that when we pray we go into the quiet of our room where no one can see us. What matters is what happens between God and us. As our children grow, they may *not* want our presence during their private prayer time; and this desire should be honored.

Some religious traditions desire their people to kneel with their hands joined and their heads raised or bowed when they pray. Other traditions encourage sitting with their heads bowed and hands folded on the lap. In still other traditions, people stand. Kneeling and standing may be difficult for some and sitting may be too comfortable and cause sleepiness for others. There is no one correct position for prayer. But there is a need for some uniformity when people gather together for worship.

What each tradition is trying to encourage is reverence. Reverence is "a feeling or attitude of deep respect, love, and awe" for the sacred.[19] Reverence is our response to the holy in our midst.

During prayer time in our homes and in our classrooms, we may choose different reverential positions from what we use during worship. We may even encourage our children to experiment with different positions and space so long as they maintain a degree of reverence. Many Sunday schools and adults have found that carpet squares or prayer rugs set up prayer space that a few minutes earlier was used for play. These carpet squares signal a change in personal demeanor and focus. If we prefer to stand, facing the East will symbolically signal a time for prayer. We may even want to dim the light. Again, there is no right or wrong way or position for approaching God. What is important is that our attention, thoughts, and conversation be directed to God and not to ourselves or with each other.

Music—Another Way to Speak to God

Music is the language of the heart. It stirs our soul. Sacred music helps open our hearts and minds to God's presence. Instead of the blare of the television all day long, sacred music could be playing softly in the background.

Some of the most awe-inspiring music is that sung by the Eastern Orthodox church choirs and the Gregorian chants sung by monks. This music is not religious entertainment. It is worshipful music. It creates and sustains an atmosphere that allows the voice of God room to speak to us.

Sacred music is part of the act of praying. We can sing to God whatever is in our hearts creating our own melody. Small children can learn simple action songs. Older children can learn simple hymns. They can sing in children's choirs. If they participate in part or all of the worship service, help them to learn to read music so that they can sing the hymns the congregation sings. If children are dismissed after the first fifteen minutes of worship, encourage your Sunday school and minister to have the singing of the same hymn several consecutive weeks, especially hymns of adoration, so that children can learn them.

Congregational hymn sings before worship are wonderful for everyone. Children can even ask to have their favorite hymn sung. Or children can have fifteen minutes of hymn singing after their classes.

Since very young children have not mastered reading, they

especially love music and poetry. They love rhythm and rhyming and find it incredibly easy to memorize simple religious music and poetry. If the music and poetry are carefully selected, they will learn several significant religious thoughts and concepts.

Church musicians are an excellent source for providing appropriate songs for children of different ages. They could record music and words so that children could sing along with a cassette tape as part of their class time.

The Larger World

Beginning around age six, children shift their focus from home to school and the larger world. Over the next several years, children's personalities begin to change. They will start the process of disengaging from us. Part of their developmental task is to become an independent human being. They may not know how to do it graciously. They may violate all our rules knowing full well that we will react.

Other people in our children's larger world begin to take on more importance. Play is no longer solitary. Playmates and mutually accepted rules have an influence on our children's behavior. Teachers and the church may be offering a different standard or set of rules than what are given or practiced at home. These outside rules or standards are important in shaping their behavior towards us and their peers and for learning how to get along outside the home.

Intellectually, cause and effect thinking develops. They seek knowledge and understanding. They do not wish to be held back in their learning. Simplistic answers to difficult questions are unacceptable. They want the resources to solve their own problems. Their minds work much like a computer organizing facts, categorizing them, and reorganizing them if necessary. They are able to memorize large amounts of information. They can tell the difference between reality and fantasy. Symbols and symbolic language such as words and mathematics take on a new importance. These initial stages of knowledge form the basis for abstract thinking which may become more dominant as early as age ten or eleven years.

Preteens' bodies begin to change. Most girls enter puberty before boys their age. Boys and girls are awkward with each other. This same awkwardness is felt among those who are more developed or less developed than the majority. Their self consciousness may also affect their emotional and intellectual lives at school and at home. Recognize and accommodate their physical and emotional crisis for what it is.

Along with their rapid intellectual and physical growth comes the need for emotional and spiritual stability in their lives. The church and the home are the two main forces influencing emotional and spiritual stability.

For our part, we need to let our children know where we stand on particular issues and what they can reasonably expect from home and from God. We need to anticipate and be ready to discuss our children's deep, penetrating questions. We need to set limits for behavior, chores, and obedience. Very often our set limits for them provide an excuse for our children when their peers pressure them to do something they wish not to do. Increasing freedom needs to be tied to responsibility. Part of the maturation process is recognizing that freedom does not come cheaply. Be selective as to what rules and behavior are acceptable and unacceptable. Pick your battles carefully. Too many skirmishes will exhaust both you and your children and will fail to distinguish the important things from the unimportant. Also remember that it is very difficult for children to go against the stream, to pit themselves against all the other children their age.

Our Christian belief will dominate how we live our lives which in turn will have an impact on how our children will live their lives.

Adolescence

Adolescence is a traumatic time for parents and their adolescents alike. Young people have gone through rapid physical growth and are self conscious of their more mature bodies. Some like the way they have become while others do not. Most are unsure of themselves. Models and movie stars establish a standard for women's and men's looks and physiques. Young people often uncritically accept these standards. Those who are too short or too tall or too thin or too heavy in comparison to these standards of beauty often have trouble accepting themselves.

In addition to accepting their bodies, adolescents are still growing intellectually. Many of them are now able to reason through and develop complicated philosophical systems and concepts. They enjoy the challenge of abstract thinking, of thinking in non-physical terms. Large numbers of our young people, however, are unwilling or incapable of thinking beyond the physical world they can see and touch.

Young people's willingness or ability to think increasingly about the unseen will also extend to their developing spirituality and their acceptance or rejection of our faith as it has been handed down to them. If we have tolerated no controversial or penetrating questions about our faith and if we have not been a part of their developing spiritual lives, they will suspect us of not being true believers.

How can we help our adolescents?

One important thing we can do is to give them spiritual and emotional growing space. That does not mean we abandon guidance and home rules. Rules reflect one form of parental love. But we have to recognize and accept their developmental need to distance themselves from us in order to grow into mature, independent adults and not clones of ourselves. Often our children will be outright defiant and belligerent toward us and all adults. And our faith and faith community become the targets of their defiance.

Some parents and teachers give up the battle for their souls before it even begins. Once their children have been confirmed and become members of the church they abdicate full spiritual responsibility for them.

Other parents and adults are alarmed by the church's benign neglect of our adolescents. They want to force upon them similar programs that they found meaningful in preceding generations. If our adolescents think their growing need for independence is constrained by these programs, they may elect to make our efforts in this direction the target of their rebellion and defiance.

Somehow we need to meet our adolescents at a midway point. Young children will not trouble themselves with the important questions of life, but adolescents will. We need to be there to address their questions and concerns. We need to have an open door policy with them. If we have a good, trusting relationship with them, they will come to us with their spiritual questions. But they will not stop with us. It is as though they need to survey everyone until they find the right combination of answers to their questions. In their own way and on their own terms, they are taking responsibility for their own spiritual lives. They are growing up.

Whatever we do, we must not pressure or impose our spiritual agenda upon our adolescents. They have enough problems moving through the turmoil of adolescence. Two possible avenues for adolescent exploration are their youth fellowship programs and Christian education classes. If they are properly conducted, they can offer a non-threatening environment in which to ask questions, especially if their leader is not a parent. Youth fellowship and Christian education classes could be some combination of discussion sessions with some fun time and outreach projects.

If you attend a church where the minister delivers sermons that resonate with adolescents, encourage them to attend church at least two times a month. Keep the sermon's message to yourself unless your adolescent wants to discuss it. Do not use the sermon as ammunition for your point of view. Revelations given to ministers often are as limited and as biased as the ones we have. Using their sermons as justification for a particular position is a kiss of death for all you hope will happen to your children in their spiritual journey.

Some of our adolescents who have grown up in homes where parents have talked about God and have prayed together may feel comfortable saying short prayers before many of their peers. If you have a group of adolescents who want to pray together, encourage them. But chances are that their prayer lives are very private. They cannot and should not be intimidated to pray out loud or on command. They may be too self conscious or not in the mood for prayer. If they are embarrassed to pray and feel forced to pray, you can be assured they will not go to their next meeting. Therefore, it is important to know the comfort level of those adolescents in your care. Silent prayer can be a good alternative to public prayer.

Proverbs and Psalms—
Two Stopping Places for Adolescents

Good stopping places for our adolescents—places that speak most to their spiritual state and needs—are the Psalms and Proverbs. Each book addresses the issues of life with its joys, sorrows, triumphs, vengeful and hateful feelings, insecurities, evil, goodness, and morality.

Proverbs falls into the literary category of Wisdom Literature that is philosophic in nature. It concerns itself with discerning the true ends and proper governance of our lives. It provides moral and religious teachings from the perspective of everyday life. The authors of Proverbs were wise men who were charged with the moral and practical training of young men from the upper classes. The teachers prepared the young men for positions of responsibility in business, politics, and diplomacy. Today women are held as accountable as men. The advice given young men in Proverbs, therefore, applies to women as well.

One governing theme of the Book of Proverbs is "The fear of the Lord is the beginning of knowledge; fools despise wisdom and instruction" (Proverbs 1:7). "Fear" means "awe." And "fools" are not the stupid ones but those "whose conduct is reprehensible."

Proverbs contains extended poems of admonition and warning, pithy maxims, and exhortations to right conduct. The entire book is filled with valuable thoughts, concepts, and discussion starters. Take for instance: "A soft answer turns away wrath, but a harsh word stirs up anger" (15:1) and "Foolish children are a grief to their father and bitterness to her who bore them" (17:25).

The Book of Psalms is considered the hymnbook and prayerbook of the Old Testament. Different people wrote psalms over several centuries. They were used in Jewish worship and have been used in Christian worship throughout the ages. There are many different types of psalms: hymns of thanksgiving, laments, royal and enthronement psalms, wisdom psalms, prayers for forgiveness, petitions for protection from and punishment of enemies, or any combination of these.

The Psalms reflect the psalmists' understanding of God's role in our lives. The psalmist exclaimed with joy, praise and thanksgiving for God's presence and self giving. He said:

> When I look at your heavens, the work of your fingers, the moon and the stars that you have established; what are human beings that you are mindful of them, mortals that you care for them? Yet you have made them a little lower than God, and crowned them with glory and honor. You have given them dominion over the works of your hands; you have put all things under their feet.
>
> Psalm 8:3-6

Psalms are prayers that are honest, sincere, sometimes joyful, and sometimes bitter. They deal openly and comprehensively with our human condition, describing it in all its rawness. The majority of these prayers show the psalmists' struggle with God, their questioning of God's actions, and how the world has treated them. The psalmists looked to God, their Creator, to redeem them from the clutches of evil. They struggled to live a life of faith and obedience. The Psalms reveal answers to the psalmists' and our personal struggles with God and with life. The Psalms reveal the dreadful pain of maturing in the faith.

Like us, the psalmists had many enemies and experiences with evil. We may either hate our enemies or repress or deny our vengeful thoughts towards them. The psalmists, however, were utterly candid with their feelings. They accused God of selling them for a pittance. One psalmist wrote: "You have sold your people for a trifle, demanding no high price for them" (Psalm 44:12).

Similar to our teenagers, one psalmist spoke of the evil their enemies bring upon innocent people. He prayed:

> Confuse, O Lord, confound their speech; for I see violence and strife in the city...and iniquity and trouble are within it; ruin is in its midst; oppression and fraud do not depart from its marketplace.
>
> Psalm 55:9-11

This same psalmist not only witnessed oppression and defrauding of the innocent, he also felt betrayed by friends. He said:

> My companion laid hands on a friend and violated a covenant with me with speech smoother than butter but with a heart set on war; with words that were softer than oil, but in fact were drawn swords.
>
> Psalm 55:20-21

All of us have experienced hostile feelings towards our enemies and despair at our friends' betrayals. We cannot and will not accept these conditions without a struggle. We bring to speech our brokenness before God. We try to talk out our emotions and our rage against the evil we encounter. We cannot but hate what violates God's creation and creatures, and we ask God to help us in righting wrongs, to take the blinders off those who could help us deal with the cancer that threatens all that is good.

We and the psalmists hope, pray, and rely on God's help. Somehow help and relief come. One psalmist prayed:

Come and hear, all you who fear God, and I will tell what he has done for me. I cried aloud to him, and he was extolled with my tongue. If I had cherished iniquity in my heart, the Lord would not have listened. But truly God has listened; he has given heed to the words of my prayer. Blessed be God, because he has not rejected my prayer or removed his steadfast love from me.

Psalm 66:16-20

The Psalms are anchored in human experience and center on God. In praying them, we turn over to God our outrage, our suffering, and our vengeance. We ask God to cleanse us of evil thoughts. We realize that bringing justice to an unjust situation does not rest solely on us. We recognize and affirm God's role in creation. Somehow God will see that justice is served and the moral order of the universe reestablished. How and when it will happen we do not know—it may not even be in our lifetime. Many innocent people may have to suffer and die before a new day is born.

The harshness of life, especially for the poor, can be unrelenting. Their employment is not guaranteed. Paychecks are stolen. Overworked parents become incapacitated. Gangs threaten with knives and guns. People living under these conditions cannot survive without a close bond of love and mutual help between the children, their families, and their parish priest or minister. Many of them identify with Jesus, with His poverty, with society's rejection of Him, and with His self-giving love. Jesus, family, and church give them *hope* not to give up and to live the best lives they can. The quality and maturity of their spiritual lives can be astounding. They truly live out Jesus' Great Love Commandment (Mark 12:29-31).

When I witness living faith in a hostile environment, I cannot help but join in with the psalmist's words: "God is our refuge and strength, a very present help in trouble" (Psalm 46:1). "Our help is in the name of the Lord, who made heaven and earth" (Psalm 124: 8).

Four Levels of Faith

John Westerhoff in his book *Will Our Children Have Faith?* uses the imagery of a tree's growth rings to suggest four different styles of faith. He reminds us that as a tree grows, it adds rings to expand and mature, but the previously formed rings are still present in the central core of the tree's trunk.

The four styles of faith Westerhoff suggests are:

Experienced Faith is the innermost ring. It is the understanding of faith through experiences such as lighting the Advent Wreath, participating in a church play, participating in the power of ritual, and sharing with the faith community. This stage of spiritual growth is similar to the early years of children. During these years we learn about God through our parents, Sunday school teachers, and other trusted adults. Simplicity and security are the hallmarks of this stage.

Affiliative Faith is the second inner ring. It is the sense of belonging to a faith community that enables one to vote at church meetings, to fill out a pledge card, and to receive adult offering envelopes. We are free to make our own decisions about what we believe, but we are also vulnerable because of our previous sheltered faith experience. Usually, however, we tend to seek the security of our peers. We tend to think similarly to our peers for fear of of being shunned by them. We enjoy the sense of belonging to a group. During this affiliative stage, many young people are insufficiently mature in their faith for independent thinking.

Searching Faith is the third and larger inner ring. As our world enlarges with age and experience, we question and doubt some of our earlier beliefs. We search for new meaning. Many people never go beyond the first two faith stages to enter the searching faith stage. Many accept and believe what they are told to believe without questioning the premises for those beliefs. If people remain in the first two faith stages, their faith remains static and without vitality. True faith, however, is alive and dynamic, not static. It is active. It is always in process. Faith struggles to answer the unanswerable questions about God and life. Faith struggles to find meaning and purpose for our lives. Faith cannot grow into a mature faith with pat answers to complex questions.

Many of us wrestled with questions of faith and identity and will continue this struggle throughout life. This searching process ultimately leads us to disengagement from our parents and church if questioning is forbidden or disencouraged by them.

I went through this trauma of disengagement by myself. My parents and church considered me a rebel because I entered the searching faith stage and said what was on my mind. I wanted the freedom to ask my own questions and to work through these questions and problems so that I could arrive at my own answers, answers which changed as new revelations came to me.

Those of you and your children who are in this searching stage need to ask your own questions and arrive at your own answers, too. Young people and adults alike need to establish their own identity in the faith community. This new identity sometimes includes some rejection or modification of previous religious and values orientation.

This disengagement is a time of transition from one form of orientation to another. Transitions are critical times of disequilibrium for parents and teenagers. Basic suppositions are discarded or others restructured. During such traumatic times our faith can grow stronger, weaker, or different.

Often parents and teachers have difficulty accepting their children's internal growth because it is unknown, embryonic, and threatening. But if the inner foundational rings of faith like the inner growth rings of a tree are well established, nothing can destroy that faith. Parents and the church should not worry; young people are going through a normal developmental stage. But if their internal faith rings are lacking this expanding searching quality, their faith may take weird twists. Many people are often turned off, as I was, by churches that do not wrestle with contemporary faith questions and issues, where people maintain an antiquarian, status quo faith. Ministers,

Christian educators, and laity are supposed to help young and old alike to interpret the Christian faith, to meet searching questions that beg for fresh explanations. Real faith is dynamic, not static.

Owned Faith is the outer ring. It is a central and vital part of a person's total being. It is the fullest expression of God's power and love in our inner being. An owned faith incorporates into our daily lives our belief and obedience to God's will. This faith is generally reached late in life. Those people in this stage have grown spiritually in ways unique to themselves and shaped by events in their lives.

Whoso shrinks from ideas ends by having nothing but sensations.

Johann Wolfgang Von Goethe

12

*

What Are the Different Types of Prayer?

As my knowledge of prayer grew, I became aware that there were many different beliefs and ways people believed they could approach God or their gods. Some of the more prominent types of prayer are primitive, ritual, philosophic, mystical, prophetic, and public communal. I will describe them below.

Primitive Prayer

Primitive prayer focuses on self and community. Entire communities pray and make sacrifices to one or more gods whom they believe are more powerful than they. Fear and self preservation are the motivating forces behind their prayers. Once people believe they have appeased their gods, they pray prayers of petition for those things they desire, prayers of in-

tercession for the well being of others, and prayers of thanksgiving for deliverance and blessings received.

Primitive prayer flatters, bargains with, pays homage, and
appeals to a god or gods' personal interests. Through sacrifices, people believe they *oblige* their gods to grant them the services and requests they make. If their gods *refuse* the people
what they want, they will seek out other gods and thereby de-
prive their gods of their devotion. These people believe *their
gods* are dependent upon them for their existence.

Coupled with this idea that gods are to render them a service is the belief that a violation of a moral code (sin) does not
govern their relationship with their gods or that this violation
will cause a possible misfortune. No thought or perceived
need is given to the need for moral regeneration.

At one time, people believed that prayer and worship became a substitute for sacrifice. Prayer and worship were
viewed as a good work that required a service from their god
in return for their personal sacrifice.

Even today many people practice some form of primitive
prayer. Let me give you an example. Mrs. G. was a devout
woman who regularly attended worship. Her worship sacrifice and devotion to God caused her to believe she deserved a
reward of continued good health and blessings. When her doc-
tor told her she had a debilitating disease, she was unable to
accept her condition and still maintain her devotion to God.
She believes she deprives God of her devotion by not attend-
ing church. She refuses to pray or allow anyone to talk to her
about God. Mrs. G. never advanced beyond this primitive
prayer level.

Ritual Prayer

We all participate at one time or another in various forms of
ritual prayer. Ritual prayer is the use of fixed language in place
of spontaneous prayer. Though ritualized prayer may seem
mechanical and devoid of the spirit of spontaneous prayer, it
often proves of great value to certain devout people who

would not pray otherwise or who would consider their prayers inadequate.

Ritual prayer is a great comfort in troubled or sorrowful times. It allows people to concentrate on the words and thoughts presented in the prayer and to go behind these words to their original freshness. The poetic beauty of Psalm 23, though considered ritual prayer, gives spiritual and emotional sustenance through its many levels of meaning. We cannot underestimate the power, imagery, and comfort of such words as: "Even though I walk through the darkest valley, I fear no evil; for you are with me; your rod and your staff—they comfort me." (See Chapter 13 for examples.)

Philosophic Prayer

Philosophic prayer has been around since the beginning of time. Those who practiced this prayer form do not worship the local gods or God. Philosophic prayer concentrates on the higher good found in life. It is prayer that has no genuine need for or communion with God. Philosophic religion constructs an ideal religion which its practitioners "hold to be true, pure, genuine, and universally valid."[20] Philosophic religion is an ideal religion that springs from pure reason wherein the notion of God is a conception of the philosopher's mind. There are no inner promptings of the soul or an awareness of God. There is no relationship with a god perceived as present or even living. Those who practice philosophic prayer believe prayer is not a necessity. Instead, for them, prayer is ethical training within the ability of people's moral power to achieve. Stoicism and asceticism are two forms of philosophic prayer.

Philosophic prayer is devoted completely to attaining a moral ideal as opposed to establishing contact with God. So when you hear people say they do not have to be a Christian, Jew, or Muslim to be a good person, they probably practice a form of philosophic prayer.

Examples of philosophic religion originated with such philosophers as Confucius, Socrates, Seneca, David Hume, Jean-Jacques Rousseau, and Immanual Kant.

Mystical Prayer

Mystical prayer has always given me problems. In my teen years, someone very close to me went into prolonged trances. She said she was praying. Maybe she was. But I thought her behavior was a cry for attention and love. Today we hear a lot about mystical prayer and getting in touch with our inner selves. Various forms of mystical prayer are uncritically accepted and practiced as a prayer technique that will bring people closer to God.

I have come to accept mystical prayer as a valid prayer form for a *limited* number of adults. But I do not believe it to be an appropriate form for our children.

Mystics believe they can achieve union with God without the use of reason and through the process of fixed meditation or spiritual exercises. They believe this union with God reveals God to them. Many mystics do not look to *revealed religion* that uses scripture as its basis and guide for faith and practice.

Mystical and prophetic prayer each form one of the two main streams for Christian spirituality. I will first discuss mystical prayer to which I am an outsider. I will then discuss prophetic prayer.

Mystical prayer is preliminary and preparatory for a mystical experience and union with God. It begins with narrowing one's focus by concentrating on a candle, a flower, a tree, or some other object. Or it can begin with the repetitious utterance of a particular prayer. The mystic meditates on this prayer. Its constant repetition has an auto-hypnotic effect. One commonly used chant: "O Lord Jesus Christ, Thou Son of God, have pity upon me!" As this chanting continues, words are no longer necessary and wordless prayer follows.

The person entering into a mystical trance will experience total isolation, silence, and withdrawal from the world. The mystic's mind moves through a progressive series of world denying attachments. This release from external things leads to a quiet and a calmness within. Thought is suspended and eventually union with God is achieved. By turning inward to commune with God who dwells within us, the mystic's soul is filled with rapture and merges into God's being.

Some scientists and psychologists think they have discovered how these mystical states occur. They have begun to investigate the effect the right and left brain hemispheres have on people's prayer. They know that the left brain controls language, logic, and the ability to conceptualize while the right brain governs our emotional states and intuition. Most people are left-brain dominant. Reason governs most of their activities. But right brain emotions such as love, joy, grief, hate, anger, sex, and reverence sometimes overpower this left-brain dominance. Psychologists believe those who practice mystical prayer have the ability to shut down their left-brain activity so completely that their right brain takes over and governs their actions.

Chemicals, hormonal imbalances, runner's high, or repetitive, rhythmic stimuli such as strobe lights, chants, and drums have been found to cause a biochemical reaction in our brain that produces an altered state of consciousness that can in turn block out outside stimuli.[21] When normal outside stimuli are consciously denied by a person's brain, especially the left brain, an altered state of consciousness occurs.

The pursuit of altered states of consciousness through autohypnotic or mystical techniques that eliminate left-brain activity may foster grave psychological difficulties.[22] Society may not be willing to accept trance-like or mystic-like states, especially in children. Modern western society may consider their behavior to be deviant and perhaps border on possession.

The mystical state is a state of passivity that has its own inherent dangers. When the mystic shelves his critical thinking faculties, there is no way to know whether the mystic is in touch with God or with some other principalities or powers. Many mystics suffer from mystical psychosis and experience a psychotic breakdown. They seek solitude and receive messages and hear voices from the spiritual world. They have no reality check that is generated by the human community and its norms. Some mystics cross over from the world of reality into a world of illusion and fantasy. They become paralyzed and exist in an inactive state.[23] Can this state be considered a true response to God?

Yet there have been some truly great Christian mystics such as St. Teresa of Avila and St. John of the Cross who have shared their experiences and insights through their writings.

Marguerite Shuster, a Presbyterian minister and a Ph.D. clinical psychologist, warns of the dangers of mystical prayer, especially for the average person. She writes:

> *Any time will and decision are relinquished, the nature and quality of relationship in which the relinquishment occurs are of critical importance.* This observation perhaps helps to explain why the bible is so restrictive about the sex act and why Christian prayer and meditation are not, biblically speaking, states of vague, blank openness. Jesus and Paul both associated prayer not with sleep or dreaminess but with watchfulness: "Watch and pray that you may not enter into temptation" (Matt. 26:41); "Continue steadfastly in prayer, being watchful in it with thanksgiving" (Col. 4:2). Prayer must *not* be confused with assorted relaxation techniques; let those who use [them] as such beware.[24]

Marguerite Shuster's studies suggest that we should avoid altered states of consciousness and mind-control techniques. Genuine prayer requires watchfulness and the full use of our mental capacity. Trance-like prayer can be harmful to children and should not be encouraged or taught to children.

Prophetic Prayer

Prophetic prayer today and in biblical times reveals people's belief that God is active in people's lives and in history. Prophetic prayer is from a biblical and historical perspective. It springs from knowledge of God learned from God's actions in our world. This knowledge is mediated through such historical witnesses as described in the Bible as well as what occurs within the faith community and through everyday events.

Throughout the Old and New Testament, we discover prayers arising out of personal needs and temptations. These prayers reflect people's needs, joys, and dependence on God. Yet there is within these prayers a powerful instinct for self preservation and a confidence and trust that God will hear them and respond to them.

In prophetic prayer, God is not believed to be a static Good as God is believed to be in mystical prayer. God is believed to be much more than Good. God is a multifaceted, incomprehensible, living, active, willing Supreme Being who seeks a loving relationship with us in our time and space, in our human history. God gives us our freedom and does not override our will. God lets us choose whether we want to be in a relationship with God or not.

The play *Fiddler on the Roof* illustrates the use of prophetic prayer. In this play, God is the reference for everything that happens in people's lives in the small, unimportant Russian town of Anatevka. Tevye, the main character and father of five daughters, is in constant conversation with God. Tevye speaks whatever is on his mind. When he thinks about his impoverished state, he asks God why God chose not to make him a rich man. He asks God: "Would it spoil some vast, eternal plan if I were a wealthy man?"[25] After such a question, it is conceivable that God laughs at his folly like a loving parent laughs at the naive requests children sometimes make to their parents.

On Tevye's daughter's wedding night, Tevye sings about the swiftness of time and the limitation of his days which are filled with joys and sorrows when he sings *Sunrise, Sunset*.

When the Jewish people are ordered to leave Anatevka during a pogrom, they are saddened but remain faithful to God. They ask the rabbi whether this time would be a good time for the Messiah to come and intervene in history. The rabbi replies: "We will have to wait for the Messiah someplace else. Meanwhile, let us start packing."[26] All the people then begin singing in a minor key about leaving their homes in Anatevka, each other, and their moving towards unknown futures.

Prophetic people take life as it comes. They believe they have an intimate, vital communion with God and that this fellowship exists in the here and now, and will exist in the future, and will last forever. This fellowship is not a blissful state or mystical union with God. God and prophetic people never merge into one. They are separate beings that remain separate yet present to each other.

Prophetic prayer is a lot like primitive prayer. It springs from emotions of great intensity such as fear, love, hate, anger, joy, grief, sex, and reverence. These emotions are spontaneous and involuntary. They are not like ideas that can be "produced by an effort of the will; their origin does not depend on us...Prayer wells up from the subconscious life of the soul."[27]

Prophetic prayer is not a product of people's egos. It is initiated and helped along by God's Holy Spirit. Prophetic prayer is personal and loving, not passive. Prophetic people actively seek to discover God's will and then to live it. They strive with God as Jacob did the night before his meeting with Esau. They may subordinate their will to God's but rarely renunciate it.

Prophetic people bring their petitions and cares to God. They may argue and struggle with God to have their way. Though the answer may be in the negative or indeterminant, there is a certain acceptance of their situation and a trust and faith in God.

Prophetic spirituality springs from revealed religion. It is social and ethical in nature. It believes and affirms life. It moves out into the world to share its message and vision with others.

Comparison of Mystical Prayer with Prophetic Prayer

Since mystical and prophetic prayer form the two main streams that influence Christian spirituality, let us compare these two prayer forms by examining the chart on the following pages which gives a summary of their major identifying characteristics.

Comparison of Mystical Prayer with Prophetic Prayer

MYSTICISM	PROPHETIC PRAYER
Love and Union with God.	**Love, faith, trust, and confidence** in god and in God's presence.
Contemplative, Passive, Silent.	**Spontaneous** response to stirring of the soul. Passionate crying and groaning, vehement complaint and pleading.
Merging of self into God.	**Distinct separation** between God and human beings. A wrestling with God.
Personality denying.	**Personality affirming**
World denying, flight from the natural world to the supernatural world. Monasticism.	**World affirming**. A great desire to live, to fight for what is moral and right, to overcome obstacles. Effort to transform the world.
Desire and embrace of Heavenly Spouse.	**Awe, humility, and reverence** before God.
Altered states of consciousness.	**Normal state of consciousness.**
God is static, undifferentiated unity and beyond normal conscious experience.[a] God is accessible only through completion of specific techniques.	**God is a multi-faceted,** living, willing Supreme Being with human emotions and personality and is always present yet independent of human beings.
Revelation *not anchored in history* and biblical history. Mystic goes beyond historical Christ because he must rid self of all images. Revelation through a direct and essential union with God.[b]	**Revelation** through God *active in history*, through God incarnate in Jesus Christ, through His sacrificial death and resurrected new life and glorification. There is "fellowship with God, in and through Christ."[c]

a Fredrich Heiler, *Prayer, A Study in the History of Religion*, trans. Samuel McComb (New York: Oxford University Press, 1932), pp. 146-47.
b Ibid., p. 152.
c Ibid.

MYSTICISM	PROPHETIC PRAYER
Knowledge derived from individual inner revelation which is non-communicable.	Divine will **revealed** through prophets and Jesus Christ.
Inner freedom from all authority.	**Personal freedom** from institutional religion.
Sin is a lust for life.	**Sin** is a violation of God's holy will.
Salvation is liberation from this world and from creaturely existence. It is achieved through the effort of the will and advancement through various steps leading to ultimate union with God.	**Salvation** is the restoration of communion with God. Salvation is an unearned gift of grace from God which cannot be earned or willed. Faith alone, which is a creative act of trust in Jesus' redemptive deeds, causes people to confess their sins, seek repentance, and the doing of God's will.
Individualistic, **non-social**.	**Social** yet individualistic. Seeks to build the faith community. Service oriented.
Immortality is an abiding vision and union with God in either a state of nirvana or ecstasy.	**Immortality** is everlasting fellowship with God that has already begun in the believer's life and grows to perfection in eternal life.
Evil—defects, deficiencies, individuality, finitude.	**Evil**—rebellion against God and God's will, God's holiness, and motivated by desire for power.
Right-brain dominant.	**Left-brain** dominant.

Mystical prayer does not spring from everyday events and history. It does not occur in the objective, historical world. It is completely individualistic in nature. Christian mystical prayer need not even be tied to Christian thinking or beliefs. A Christian mystic's devotion to Jesus is considered by many to be only a *means* for achieving union with God.

Mystics elect passivity and reject the gift of free will. This elected passivity makes an individual seem like God's robot without free will. And yet most Christians believe God has given us free will. How we use our free will is our choice.

Some mystics steeped in scripture do not lose sight of God's purposes. Catherine of Siena spoke the Word of the Lord given to her in an ecstatic vision. She said:

> It is impossible for you to give me the love that I ask, but I have given you a neighbor that you may do for him that which you cannot do for me. Love him without any worldly thought, without looking for any gain or return. That which you do for him, I look upon as done for me.

No one prayer form should dominate our prayer lives. In fact, there are positives and negatives regarding each form used. For instance, if prophetic prayer is carried to extremes, it often becomes harsh, judgmental, over zealous, and severe. It can be grave and penitential in tone. It may lack the most precious element of mystical prayer of intimacy with God, love for Christ and surrender. Prophetic prayer can degenerate into an ethical and utilitarian belief. Yet prophetic prayer in its simplicity most resembles the release of our inborn passions and human feelings. It is not a state which we have to induce.

In order to know and experience Jesus in our hearts, we need to appropriate and merge some of the better features of mystical prayer with the better prayer features of prophetic prayer. It is important that we bring to speech what is in our heart and talk about it, either silently or aloud, with God from whom we seek comfort and help. We do not want to become like the Pharisees and scribes who knew the Law thoroughly but did not let it be written on their hearts. Our prayer lives need to be free from total self-absorption so that we can be open to God's revelation, message, and presence. Our lives should reflect the fruits of the Spirit and our identification with God's will in showing love, service, and compassion towards our neighbors.

Public Communal Prayer

God created us for fellowship with each other and with God. We are not meant to live alone. Therefore, we live and govern ourselves into some form of political entity as well as into various faith communities.

A worshipping community gathers together to hear scripture read and interpreted followed by communal prayers and often the celebration of the eucharist. Awe, wonder, and praise seize us and bind us to each other and to God. We come to view God's world through God's point of view. Congregations often participate verbally in communal prayer either through responsive or unison prayer. These two forms of prayer usually precede the sermon and the pastoral prayer. God speaks to us through the reading of God's word and the interpretation of that word through the sermon. Following the sermon, we speak to God through the pastoral prayer. This prayer should be the high point of the worship service.

Sometimes we may witness ostentatious displays of prayer in our faith community. Jesus severely condemned these displays as impure prayer.

Prayer for Children

As our children's principal spiritual leaders, it is important that we take into account their personality and learning style. Some of them learn visually, some auditorily, some through intellectual pursuits, and some through a hands-on approach. They all have different personalities, come from different environments, and have different needs. Some of them are introverts and shy while others are extroverts.

When it comes to what type of prayer is best for children, it is best to introduce them to the various types and let them choose which type or combinations best agree with their personality, learning style, age and ability, and place in their spiritual journey. *Our main purpose is to help them to be in communication with God.* (See Chapter 13 for various categories of prayers.)

For instance, the beauty of mystical prayer is the act of mental withdrawal from the distractions of this world and concentration on God. Abrupt interruption from our busy lives for a moment of prayer has its place, too, especially during times of crisis. This momentary disruption does not allow us time to rid our minds of distractions. Mystical prayer, however, recognizes the need for inner quiet so as to open all our communication channels to God.

I do not think it advisable for children and young people to travel the full road to mysticism that leads to an altered state of consciousness. Only the act of quiet time with God is suggested for children and nothing more. Let us take seriously psychologists' warnings about the inherent dangers to the human psyche with altered states of consciousness.

Ritual prayer serves an important function in helping children develop a prayer life, provided children concentrate on the meaning of the words in these prayers. These words should stimulate children's thoughts and help them communicate with God on a deeper and more personal level.

Communal prayer is a shared worship experience that should heighten children's sense of belonging to a faith community where everyone stands in an equal relationship to each other and as part of the whole faith community in God's presence and in communion with God.

As communal prayer helps make us aware of our connectedness to each other and to God, so also does prophetic prayer with its emphasis on people's past and present experiences with God in their history. This prayer form most nearly represents children's social experiences that activate heartfelt emotions within them that naturally well up into prayer. With their growing knowledge and understanding of the Bible, children and young people should be able to pray for God's help in making difficult Christian decisions that have had precedent in time and space, in history. Let us encourage them to carry on a natural conversation with God.

All the doors that lead inward, to the sacred place of the Most High, are doors outward— out of self, out of smallness, out of wrong.

George MacDonald

*

I know now that patriotism is not enough; I must have no hatred and no bitterness toward anyone.

Edith Cavell
English nurse, before her execution
by Germans in World War I

13

*

Sample Prayers

Getting children, especially older children, to initiate praying will be a challenge. This chapter introduces different categories of prayers, insights on them, and sample prayers for illustrating them. There is no prescription for talking to God. What I am trying to give you here and throughout this book is the *key* to understanding prayer. You and your children must open the door and travel the spiritual journey together. Hopefully, this book will help guide you and your children and make you feel more at ease praying.

Children learn by doing. If they are given a sample prayer and asked to write a similar prayer with their own thoughts and words, they will soon be able to compose their own prayers without any samples. Writing and rewriting prayers help them clarify their thoughts and give them a critical understanding of prayer. Therefore, I strongly suggest that you copy various prayers from this chapter or from various books on prayer and use them as springboards for new prayers for your children. You may wish to begin with the Lord's Prayer. Over the next few years, if your children develop prayers that might benefit others, please send them to me with their permission to include it in a book of children's prayers.

Adoration

If we are to help our children in their prayer lives, we need to help them turn their complete attention to God and keep it free from distractions. It is important that they learn that prayer is communication and conversation with God and that they can conduct only one conversation at a time. Remind them that God is always present to them but they sometimes may not be aware of God's presence.

Tell them that prayer begins with God and not with themselves. Most children are preoccupied with self, and it is only natural for them to come to God with their thoughts and needs. God wants to hear them. But first, as in the Lord's Prayer, it is important to pause and know to whom they are speaking.

Generally speaking, the structure of a good prayer includes a portion devoted to adoration. Adoration includes the dimension of awe, wonder, and reverence. It contemplates God's glory, goodness, and mercy. It is an act of self surrender and a recognition of God's greatness, power, and divine nature. Adoration helps keep God central in our prayers.

It is important, therefore, that children learn to express their adoration of God not to influence God but to focus their attention on God. God's trail can be easily found in the wonders of nature and in the scientific unlocking of many of nature's secrets.

Young Children

With very young children, you may want to try a responsive, open-ended prayer such as the one that follows:

Adult: God, I know you are wonderful.
You are my special guide.
I know you are with me when_____.
Thank you for_____.

Child: Thank you for my_____(dog, cat).
         Thank you for my_____(blanket, doll, friends).

Adult: I tried to do good things today when I_____.

Child: I _____(helped mommy, made my bed).

All: Be with us_____(today, tonight, tomorrow). Amen.

Or you may want to help your children make up simple prayers of adoration based on the concrete wonders they can feel, touch, see, taste, and hear in their lives. Here are some examples I wrote. Feel free to use or adapt them.

Dear God, You are good and love all you have made.
I am your child. Help me to love you and everybody. Amen.

✳

God, you made me and the world.
How great you must be.
You made my mommy, my daddy, my baby brother, and me.
Thank you for everything you have given me.
Help me to be good. Amen.

✳

Dear God, You are wonderful
You made day and night.
I love the day for........(playing).
I love the night for...... (dreaming and sleeping).
Thank you. Amen.

✳

Dear God, I see the moon and stars
And wonder where you are.
Are you in my room tonight?
Or are you watching me from
Some far away star?
Be with me tonight. Good night!

＊

Dear God, Your sun is shining.
Your birds are chirping.
It is time to wake up
And to say thank you for this new day. Amen.

＊

O God, what a beautiful redbird!
It sings its song to you and to me.
It wakes me up in the morning.
Thank you for all of the pretty birds! Amen.

＊

Dear Jesus, Did you have a teddy bear like mine?
Was he cuddly and soft?
Did he smell nice?
I love my teddy and I love you. Amen.

＊

O God, today I woke up and saw everything covered
 with pretty white snow.
When I put my foot in it, my boot made a footprint.
Then I laid in it and made an angel by moving my arms and legs.
We went sleigh riding, too. And oh, what fun it was.
Thank you God for this day and the snow. Amen.

Older children

The Bible is filled with wonderful quotations of people's
adoration and understanding of God. Older children should
become familiar with these prophetic prayers and statements.
Inclusive language is used with these verses. From our children's growing understanding of God and from these model
verses, they can make up their own prayers of adoration.

For the Lord your God is God of gods, the great God, mighty
and awesome, who is not partial and takes no bribe, who exe-
cutes justice for the orphan and the widow, and who loves the
strangers, providing them food and clothing.

Deuteronomy 10:17

✳

Great is our God, and greatly to be praised;
God's greatness is unsearchable.

Psalm 145:3

✳

I am God and no mortal, the Holy One in your midst.

Hosea 11:9

✳

Have you not known? Have you not heard?
The Lord is the everlasting God,
   the Creator of the ends of the earth.
God does not faint or grow weary;
   God's understanding is unsearchable.
God gives power to the faint,
   and strengthens the powerless.
Even youths will faint and be weary,
   and the young will fall exhausted;
      but those who wait for God shall renew their strength,
      they shall mount up with wings like eagles,
      they shall run and not be weary,
      they shall walk and not faint.

                                        Isaiah 40:28-31

*

The sun shall no longer be your light by day,
   nor for brightness
   shall the moon give light to you by night;
   but God will be your everlasting light,
   and your God will be your glory.

                                        Isaiah 60:19

*

For great is God, and greatly to be praised;
   God is to be revered above all gods.
For all the gods of the peoples are idols,
   but our God made the heavens.
Honor and majesty are before God;
   strength and joy belong to God.

                                        I Chronicles 16:25-27

*

For it was you who formed my inward parts;
  you knit me together in my mother's womb.
I praise you, for I am fearfully and wonderfully made.
Wonderful are your works; that I know very well.
My frame was not hidden from you,
  when I was being made in secret,
  intricately woven in the depths of the earth.
Your eyes beheld my unformed substance.
In your book were written all the days
  that were formed for me,
  when none of them as yet existed.
How weighty to me are your thoughts, O God!
How vast is the sum of them!
I try to count them—they are more than the sand,
I come to the end—I am still with you.

Psalm 139:13-18

❋

Seek God while God may be found,
  call upon God while God is near;
  let the wicked forsake their way,
  and the unrighteous their thoughts;
  let them return to God, that God may have mercy on them,
  for God will abundantly pardon,
For God's thoughts are not our thoughts,
  nor are our ways God's ways.
For as the heavens are higher than the earth,
  so are God's ways higher than our ways and God's
  thoughts than our thoughts.

Isaiah 55:6-9

Another inspiring prayer is Paul's famous Areopagus speech about God to an Athenian crowd.

Athenians, I see how extremely religious you are in every way. For as I went through the city and looked carefully at the objects of your worship, I found among them an altar with the inscription, "To an unknown god." What therefore you worship as unknown, this I proclaim to you. The God who made the world and everything in it, is Lord of heaven and earth and does not live in shrines made by human hands, nor is served by human hands, as though God needed anything, since God gives to all mortals life and breath and all things. From one ancestor God made all nations to inhabit the whole earth, and God allotted the times of their existence and the boundaries of the places where they would live, so that they would search for God and perhaps grope for God and find God—though indeed God is not far from each one of us. For "In God we live and move and have our being"; as even some of your own poets have said, "For we too are God's offspring."

Since we are God's offspring, we ought not to think that the deity is like gold, or silver, or stone, an image formed by the art and imagination of mortals. While God has overlooked the times of human ignorance, now God commands all people everywhere to repent, because God has fixed a day on which God will have the world judged in righteousness by a man whom God has appointed, and of this God has given assurance to all by raising him from the dead.

Acts 17:22-23

Music is the language of the heart. Hymns are prayers and poetic language set to music. They awaken us to God's presence and lift our souls above the mundane. Many excellent prayers of adoration can be found in hymn and prayer books. By studying how they are formed, it is possible to create personal prayers of adoration.

Holy, Holy, Holy! Lord God Almighty!

Holy, holy, holy! Lord God Almighty!
Early in the morning our song shall rise to you;
Holy, holy, holy! merciful and mighty;
God in three persons, blessed Trinity!

Holy, holy, holy! though the darkness hide you,
Though the eye of sinful man your glory may not see;
Only you are holy; there is none beside you,
Perfect in power, in love, and purity.

Holy, holy, holy! Lord God Almighty!
All your works shall praise your name
    in earth and sky and sea;
Holy, holy, holy! merciful and mighty;
God in three persons, blessed Trinity! Amen.

✳

Ancient of Days, Who Sittest Throned in Glory

O holy Jesus, Prince of peace and Savior,
To you we owe the peace that still prevails,
Stilling the rude wills of men's wild behavior,
And calming passion's fierce and stormy gales.

O Holy Ghost, the Lord and the Life-giver,
Thine is the quickening power that gives increase;
From you have flowed, as from a pleasant river,
Our plenty, wealth, prosperity, and peace.

O Triune God, with heart and voice adoring
Praise we the goodness that doth crown our days;
Pray we that you will hear us, still imploring
Your love and favor, kept to us always. Amen.

✻

Immortal, Invisible, God only Wise,

Immortal, invisible, God only wise,
In light inaccessible hid from our eyes,
Most blessed, most glorious, the Ancient of Days,
Almighty, victorious, your great name we praise.

Unresting, unhasting, and silent as light,
Nor wanting, nor wasting, you rulest in might;
Your justice like mountains high soaring above
Your clouds which are fountains of goodness and love.

To all, life you givest to both great and small;
In all life you livest, the true life of all;
We blossom and flourish as leaves on the tree,
And wither and perish, but naught changeth thee.

Creator of glory, Creator of light,
Your angels adore you, all veiling their sight;
All praise we would render; O help us to see
'Tis only the splendor of light hideth thee. Amen.

✻

O God, when I look at the volume and might of our great salt waters and the power of a majestic waterfall and realize that you formed them and separated them from dry land with nothing more than your voice, I tremble and stand in awe of you.

Who am I that you care about me? Yet Jesus tells us you love us and that even the hair on our head is numbered by you.

Help me to grow in my understanding of your ways. Help me to see what the eyes cannot see and the ears cannot hear. And then use my voice as your voice and my hands as your hands and may they be further witness of your glory. Amen.

A.E.K.

＊

To you, O Supreme God, belongs all power and glory.
To you, O Supreme God, belongs all adoration
    and thankfulness.
You came as one of us, as a little baby in a manger.
You took on our humanity and lived our life.
Through Jesus, you explained your ways to us.
Jesus brought good news to the poor, release to the captives,
    sight to the blind, and freedom to the oppressed.
For us, you let Jesus suffer and die on a hated cross
    to show us what evil we can unleash.
And then you showed us your power and glory.
You showed us that evil will have its dark hour
    for only a short time.
But surely as day follows night, life will follow death.
And then evil will have no power over us.
For thine is the kingdom, the power,
    and the glory forever. Amen.

A.E.K.

One problem we encounter in studying other people's prayers is their seeming perfection in construction. This perfection may be an obstacle to our children's prayers. Encourage young people to speak or write from their heart. It is to God and God alone to whom they speak and write. There is no right or wrong way to carry on this conversation. Their language usage may not be perfect either. God wants them to be natural and have no artifice. Their prayers should reflect their personalities and way of speaking. Sample prayers are good for meditation and models for their own prayers. They do not set the standard language for prayer and what is in someone's heart.

Petition and Intercession

Prayers of petition cover ours and other people's mental, physical, emotional, and spiritual needs. Young people need to learn to go to God with their anxieties for which help and relief are sought.

Their motives for what they ask are as important as their requests. All their thoughts can be expressed in prayer, but their requests and petitions should be made with the reservation that they be for their ultimate good and in accordance with God's will. As stated earlier in the Lord's Prayer under the petition "Thy kingdom come," God's will is unity, peace, wholeness, joy, goodness, righteousness, purity, fidelity, love, hope, and faithfulness. If young people believe that God's will should be done, then they are in no position to tell God what God's will ought to be. Their petitions need to be in harmony with God's will.

Their petitions can be put into three concentric circles. In the inner circle, they can place all those requests they know God will give them, such as spiritual blessings and strength. Jesus made it very clear that God would answer these petitions when He said: "Ask, and it will be given you; search, and you will find; knock, and the door will be opened for you" (Matthew 7:7). In the middle circle, they can place all those temporal and spiritual blessings which may or may not be God's will to give them, such as good health, material wealth, and success. In the outer circle, they can place all those things they know are not in accordance with God's will and for which it is wrong to pray, such as revenge, hate, and success for dishonest practices.[28]

An examination of worship books and books on prayer reveals that almost all prayers of petition concentrate on relationships, attitudes, and motivations. These petitionary prayers all seek to make others and ourselves whole and integrated Christians mentally, physically, emotionally, and spiritually. Perhaps the most famous prayer of petition that illustrates this concept is a prayer attributed to St. Francis of Assisi. In this prayer, St. Francis seeks self improvement through a positive attitude and action.

> Lord, make me an instrument of your peace. Where there is hatred, let me sow love; where there is injury, pardon; where there is doubt, faith; where there is despair, hope; where there is sadness, joy; where there is darkness, light.

> O Divine Master, grant that I may not so much seek to be consoled, as to console; not so much to be understood, as to understand; not so much to be loved, as to love. For it is in giving that we receive, it is in pardoning that we are pardoned, it is in dying that we are born again to eternal life.

When teaching young people petitionary prayers, it is important to emphasize spiritual gifts and knowledge and not unnecessary material gifts. The petition Jesus taught us in the Lord's Prayer of "Give *us* this day *our* daily bread" emphasizes all people's mutual need for the essentials of life. All of our abundance needs to be shared with others. Our daily bread and all that may be interpreted under that phrase are to be used to strengthen, protect, and nourish our body and our spiritual lives. Very young children are accustomed to asking us for something and getting their desires granted a good percentage of the time. If we want to play Santa Claus, so be it.

But God does not play Santa Claus. Perhaps the most difficult lesson young children need to learn is to think beyond themselves. Therefore, it is important to teach them prayers of petition that include them but also focus on people beyond the immediate family and friends.

Young Children

Encourage *very young children* to keep their prayers short and their thoughts focused on God, concerns in their universe, and other people. Very young children can use my prayers that follow. These prayers can also form the skeletal framework for older children's prayer.

Good morning, Jesus.
Thank you for this new day.
I am going to run and play.
Please be with me all day. Amen.

❋

O God, this beach is so pretty.
I love the feel of sand in my hands.
I love to run barefooted in the sand.
I want to build a big sand castle.
Help me to share my bucket and shovel
With other little children like me. Amen.

❋

Dear Jesus, I do not feel very well today.
I woke up with a sore throat.
Help me, if it is your will,
    to get well soon.
If I am to be sick for a little longer,
    help me to be cheerful. Amen.

❋

Dear Jesus,
I got _____'s chicken pox.
The pimples itch so badly.
Help me not to scratch.
Teach me to be patient.
And may I get well soon. Amen.

❉

Lord Jesus,
You are my friend.
Be with me today. Amen.

❉

Lord Jesus,
Nursery school starts today.
I want to go but I am afraid.
Will my teachers like me?
Will the other children be nice to me?
Help me to be unafraid and to like everyone. Amen.

❉

Dear God,
It is time for me to go to sleep.
Be with me through the night.
Be with mommy, daddy,_____,too. Amen.

❉

Dear Jesus,
I am very sad tonight.
My (friend, pet, sister) died today.
I loved him very much.
He was very good_____.
And now he is with you.
Take good care of him.
And help me not to be so sad. Amen.

*

O dear God, the thunder and lightning frighten me.
Help me be brave and not to scream in fright. Amen.

*

Dear God, Freckles got himself dirty today.
Mommy was not happy about it.
She wouldn't let a dirty dog in the house.
She said I would have to clean him up
if he were to come into our house.
Freckles does not like to be cleaned by me.
He will not stand still.
He is too big for me to clean by myself.
He ran away from me.
Now he has to spend the night in the garage.
Tomorrow Mommy says she will clean him.
Help me to teach Freckles to stay clean.
I love Freckles and I love you. Amen.

Older Children

Grade school children can model their petitionary prayers on the preceding ones but in expanded form. They can also add words of adoration and confession.

O God, today we visited cousin_____in the country.
It is very lonely out there.
And I did not like the games they played.
Then we went fishing and that was worst of all.
Why do we like such different things?
Cousin_____will visit me in the city.
Help me to understand cousin_____'s way of life.
Help cousin_____to understand how we live. Amen.

A.E.K.

✳

Dear God, You made us a beautiful world.
You showed us how to build villages and cities.
Today, I rode on the train with Mommy to the city.
I saw a lot of kids playing in the streets.
You made us all and I know you love us.
But why do these kids not have green grass to play on?
Help me to understand their way of living.
Help me to be a friend to city kids. Amen.

A.E.K.

✳

Lord Jesus, you are strong and brave.
Yet you let evil people kill you. And you forgave them.
Today, _____ kicked me and said some mean things.
I almost could hate _____. Forgive me for such feelings.
How can I be a good Christian and not let _____ push me
around?
Give me the courage and strength to stand up to _____.
Help me to defend myself.
Help me not to hate or seek revenge.
Help me to forgive _____.
Show me the way. Amen.

A.E.K.

✳

O God, you are our guide and protector.
Daddy is (driving, flying) far away from here.
Please bless and protect him.
Please bring him home safely to us. Amen.

A.E.K.

Adolescents

Adolescent prayers of petition should reflect a deepening
understanding of God's ways and purpose for their lives.
Many Psalms and prayers from the Bible as well as other people's prayers are good prayers on which to meditate before ut-
tering their own prayers.

O God, You sent Jesus and the prophets to show us
How to live a healthy, spirit-filled life.
We ask that you heal our minds, our bodies and our spirits.

Help give us healthy bodies. Let us not abuse them through lack of exercise and sleep, poor eating habits, and misuse of alcohol and drugs.

Help us abandon all bad habits that would prevent us from living full, productive lives in your service. Help us remember that our bodies are the temple for the Holy Spirit within us, that we are Christ's, and that our bodies are not our own. For they were bought with a price; therefore we should glorify Christ in our bodies.

Help give us healthy minds. Jesus taught us the way to keep our minds healthy when He gave us the Great Love Commandment. He said: "Hear, O Israel: the Lord our God, the Lord is one; you shall love the Lord your God with all your heart, and with all your soul, and with all your mind and with all your strength...You shall love your neighbor as yourself." May our love for you keep our mind on you, O God, and on service to you.

Help us keep sordid, evil, and dishonorable thoughts from finding a dwelling place in our minds. Help us seek and uphold truth. Help us not to be anxious about those things which we cannot change. Give us the strength and courage to change those things which need to be changed for the betterment of everyone.

Help us develop our spiritual lives. At our baptism our parents and ministers prayed that your Spirit would comfort and guide us all the days of our lives. Stay with us, Holy Spirit, and let not unclean spirits tempt us and possess us. Cleanse us and rid us of all that would diminish us in your sight and prevent us from serving you.

We ask these things so our lives can be used to your service and in the name of Jesus Christ our Lord. Amen.

A.E.K.

O God, give my spirit power to climb the hills
And to descend into the valleys where you call me.
Let me not mistake my desires as your desire for me.
Be a quiet resting place for my soul when it is troubled.
Help me always to remember that to adore you is to love you,
To love you is to obey you. You are my companion on my
    spiritual journey and the end of my journey. Amen.

A.E.K.

*

O Lord God of time and eternity,
    who makes us creatures of time
that, when time is over,
    we may attain your blessed eternity;
With time, your gift,
    give us also wisdom to redeem the time
    lest our day of grace be lost;
    for our Lord Jesus' sake. Amen.

Christina Rossetti

*

Almighty, God, from whom all thoughts of truth and peace proceed; kindle, we pray you, in the hearts of all the true love of peace; and guide with your pure and peaceable wisdom those who take counsel for the nations of the earth; that in tranquility your kingdom may go forward, till the earth be filled with the knowledge of your love; through Jesus Christ our Lord. Amen.

Frances Paget

❋

Father, if you are willing, remove this cup from me;
    yet not my will but yours be done.

Luke 22:42

❋

Father, forgive them; for they know not what they are doing.

Luke 23:34

❋

Lord, you know everyone's heart. Show us which one of these two you have chosen to take the place in this ministry and apostleship from which Judas turned aside to go to his own place.

Acts 1:25

When reading a psalm, remember the second line is an explanation or an expansion of the first line in a couplet.

O Lord my God, in you I take refuge;
  save me from all my pursuers, and deliver me,
or like a lion they will tear me apart;
  they will drag me away, with no one to rescue.

O Lord my God, if I have done this,
  if there is wrong in my hands,
if I have repaid my ally with harm
  or plundered my foe without cause,
then let the enemy pursue and overtake me,
    trample my life to the ground,
    and lay my soul in the dust.

Rise up, O Lord, in your anger;
  lift yourself up against the fury of my enemies;
  awake, O my God; you have appointed a judgment.
Let the assembly of the peoples be gathered around you,
  and over it take your seat on high.
The Lord judges the peoples;
  judge me, O Lord, according to my righteousness
  and according to the integrity that is in me.

O let the evil of the wicked come to an end,
  but establish the righteous,
you who test the minds and hearts,
  O righteous God.
God is my shield,
  who saves the upright in heart.
God is a righteous judge,
  and a God who has indignation every day.

If one does not repent, God will whet his sword;
   he has bent and strung his bow;
he has prepared his deadly weapons,
   making his arrows fiery shafts.
See how they conceive evil,
   and are pregnant with mischief,
   and bring forth lies.
They make a pit, digging it out,
   and fall into the hole that they have made.
Their mischief returns upon their own heads,
   and on their own heads their violence descends.

I will give to the Lord the thanks
   due to the Lord's righteousness,
   and sing praise to the name of the Lord, the Most High.

Psalm 7

✳

O God, merciful and great, hear my prayer.
My body is sick and my mind is sorely distressed.
Doctors and nurses hover over me day and night.
My parents and friends whisper about me.
Will I get well?
Will I once again have the strength to live a full life?
Please, do not let me despair.
Give me patience, courage and strength
   to endure my pain and suffering.
Forgive me for all my sins. Have mercy upon me.
Restore me to health, if it be your will.
If not, let me dwell eternally with you. Amen.

A.E.K.

✳

O most knowing God, Creator of the universe and of all people,
You look upon your creation and must be joyful
   about some people's doings and saddened about others.
Help us to stop our self-seeking and warring ways.
Open our eyes to see what can be done
   and then give us strength to do it.
Help us to love and do good toward those
   who seem to us unlovable.
Help us to appreciate and respect people's differences.
Protect us all from evil doers, hatred, and revenge.
Guide us in your ways and
   give us confidence that you will always give us
   the necessary strength, comfort, and courage
   we need in trying times. Amen.

A.E.K.

✳

We most humbly beg you to give us grace not only to be hearers of the Word, but doers also of the same; not only to love, but also to live your gospel; not only to favor, but also to follow your godly doctrine; not only to profess, but also to practice your blessed commandments, to the honor of your Holy Name, and the health of our souls.

Thomas Becon

✳

Into your hands, O merciful Savior, we commend the soul of your servant now departed from the body. Acknowledge, we humbly beg you, a sheep of your own fold, a lamb of your own flock, a sinner of your own redeeming. Receive him into the arms of your mercy, into the blessed rest of everlasting peace and into the glorious company of the saints in light.

John Cosin

✳

Speak, Lord, for your servant hears.
Grant us ears to hear,
Eyes to see,
Wills to obey,
Hearts to love;
Then declare what You will,
Reveal what You will,
Command what You will,
Demand what You will. Amen.

Christina Rossetti

＊

Dear God, be with me today.
Guide me through the darkness and pitfalls of life.
Help me climb into the light of your world and your love.
Let me not seek revenge against those who wound me.
Let me spend my pain and anger in constructive ways,
    so that your peace, your justice, and your mercy may reign.
Help me balance and control my hate
    for that which oppresses and harms others
    with your love that understands my anger and heals my
    wounds.
Teach me to trust, hope, love, and to forgive
    as Jesus did. Amen.

A.E.K.

＊

O God, you make all things new and right within me if I ask.
Help me to face reality. Let me not spend all my time and energy denying there is a problem. I fear change and being discriminated against. If I acknowledge that my friends and I exploit others for our advantage, my friends will deny me. My denial of this exploitation is also a denial of you. Give me courage and spiritual strength to take responsibility for my own actions and actions towards others. Give me the courage to do your will and to encourage others to do your will. Amen.

A.E.K.

O God, be with me today.
Guide me safely through those obstacles that can ensnare me.
Help me avoid the dark side of life.
Teach me to seek only the light of your world and your love.
Help me to be an instrument of your peace.
Let me not be afraid of those who oppose your will
   and who oppress and destroy the helpless.
Let me not seek revenge against those who do me and others
   wrong.
Teach me to spend my pain and anger in constructive ways
   so that your peace, your justice, your mercy, and your heal-
   ing may reign. Amen.

A.E.K.

✳

Two things I ask of you;
   do not deny them to me before I die:
Remove far from me falsehood and lying;
   give me neither poverty nor riches;
   feed me with the food that I need,
   or I shall be full, and deny you,
   and say, "Who is the Lord?"
   or I shall be poor, and steal,
   and profane the name of my God.

Proverbs 30:7-9

Thanksgiving

It is important that our children learn prayers of thanksgiving. These prayers are our and hopefully will be their natural response to God's many gifts and to life itself. These prayers acknowledge our dependence upon God in all circumstances including good and bad situations.

Teach our children prayers of thanksgiving. Help them name the gifts for which we are thankful. Naming gives them a sense of the sacramental meaning of life. They will come to understand blessings as signs of God's mercy and our sufferings as being within God's power to use for our good even though we may not be able at any given time to accept them gratefully. Christian joy even under adverse circumstances is founded in the saving work of Jesus Christ.

Thanksgiving differs from adoration. Adoration contemplates God's glory, mercy, and goodness. Thanksgiving recognizes a Giver and those who benefit from God's actions and mercy. Thanksgiving is acceptance and acknowledgment of the gift from the Giver.

Christian joy comes when we recognize and love the Giver more than we appreciate the gift. This nation's Thanksgiving testifies to such love and recognition.

It is told that when the New England Colonies were first planted, the settlers endured many privations and difficulties. Being piously disposed, they laid their distresses before God in frequent days of fasting and prayer. Constant meditation on such topics kept their minds gloomy and discontented, and made them disposed even to return to their Fatherland with all its persecutions. At length, when it was proposed to appoint a day of fasting and prayer, a plain, common-sense old colonist was in the meeting, and remarked that he thought they had brooded long enough over their misfortunes, and that it seemed high time they should consider some of their mercies—that the colony was growing strong, the fields increasing in harvests, the rivers full of fish, and the woods of game, the air sweet, the climate salubrious, and their homes happy; above all, that they possessed what they came for, full civil and religious liberty.

And therefore, on the whole, he would amend their resolution for a fast, and propose in its stead a day of thanksgiving. His advice was taken, and from that day to this the festival has been an annual one.[29]

With young people of all ages, grace before meals is a good time to express our gratefulness to God and love for God. It is a special time when we break bread together and share our love, our joy, and our concerns with each other. It is also a good time to name our particular blessings. Table blessings can be as simple as:

God is great. God is good.
And we thank God for our food.

Or young people may wish to add the remainder of this prayer.

By God's hand we all are fed;
Give us, God, our daily bread.
Bless our home with peace and love,
And grant in Christ a home above!
For these and all God's mercies
May God's holy name be praised. Amen.

*

O Heavenly Creator, You have filled the world with beauty, we ask you to open our eyes to behold your gracious hand in all your works; that rejoicing in your whole creation, we may learn to serve you with gladness.

Book of Common Prayer (Variation)

*

Come, dear Lord, be our guest.
We thank you for the food we are about to eat.
We thank you for_____ (food to be consumed).
We thank you for nourishing our bodies, minds, and spirits.
Teach us to be the people we are meant to be.
Help us keep our faith and trust in you. Amen.

                                                    A.E.K.

*

Our God, you are the final source of all our comforts and to you we give thanks for this food. But we also remember in gratitude the many men and women whose labor was necessary to produce it and who gathered it from the land and afar from the sea for our sustenance. Grant that they too may enjoy the fruit of their labor without want, and may be bound up with us in a fellowship of thankful hearts.

                                        Walter Rauschenbusch

After most prayers of petition in the Psalms, there is a prayer of thanksgiving. For example, Psalm 109 is a vehement cry for deliverance from one's personal enemies. After stating his case, the psalmist believes God has heard his cry and concludes with these words of thanksgiving:

With my mouth I will give great thanks to the Lord;
   I will praise God in the midst of the throng.
For God stands at the right hand of the needy,
   to save them
   from those who would condemn them to death.

                                        Psalm 109:30-31

*

Other psalms, such as Psalm 100, are solely prayers of thanksgiving.

Make a joyful noise to the Lord, all the earth.
Worship the Lord with gladness;
come into the Lord's presence with singing.

Know that the Lord is God.
It is God that made us, and we are God's;
we are God's people, and the sheep of God's pasture.

Enter God's gates with thanksgiving,
and God's courts with praise.
Give thanks to God, bless God's name.

For God is good;
God's steadfast love endures forever,
and God's faithfulness to all generations.

*

Some other biblical expressions of thanksgiving are:

It is good to give thanks to the Lord
to sing praises to your name, O Most High.

Psalm 92:1

*

Rejoice in the Lord always; again I will say, Rejoice. Let your gentleness be known to everyone. The Lord is near. Do not worry about anything, but in everything by prayer and supplication with thanksgiving let your requests be made known to God. And the peace of God, which surpasses all understanding, will guard your hearts and your minds in Christ Jesus.

Philippians 4:4-7

When Paul arrived in Rome to stand trial, other Christians traveled to meet him. The book of Acts says: "On seeing them, Paul thanked God and took courage" (Acts 28:15).

Hymns are another source for prayers of thanksgivings. Some follow.

Come, Ye Thankful People, Come

Come, ye thankful people, come,
Raise the song of harvest home;
All is safely gathered in
Ere the winter storms begin;
God, our Maker, doth provide
For our wants to be supplied;
Come to God's own temple, come,
Raise the song of harvest home.

All the blessings of the field,
All the stores the gardens yield,
All the fruits in full supply,
Ripened 'neath the summer sky,
All that spring with bounteous hand
Scatters o'er the smiling land,
All that liberal autumn pours
From her rich o'er-flowing stores,

These to thee, our God, we owe,
Source whence all our blessings flow;
And for these our souls shall raise
Grateful vows and solemn praise.
Come, then, thankful people, come,
Raise the song of harvest home;
Come to God's own temple, come,
Raise the song of harvest home. Amen.

✳

For the Beauty of the Earth

For the beauty of the earth, For the beauty of the skies,
For the love which from our birth Over and around us lies,
Lord of all, to thee we raise This our hymn of grateful praise.

For the beauty of each hour Of the day and of the night,
Hill and vale, and tree and flower,
Sun and moon, and stars of light,
Lord of all, to thee we raise This our hymn of grateful praise.

For the joy of ear and eye, For the heart and mind's delight,
For the mystic harmony Linking sense to sound and sight,
Lord of all, to thee we raise This our hymn of grateful praise.

For the joy of human love, Brother, sister, parent, child,
Friends on earth, and friends above,
For all gentle thoughts and mild,
Lord of all, to thee we raise This our hymn of grateful praise.

For each perfect gift of thine Unto us so freely given,
Graces, human and divine, Flowers of earth and buds of heaven,
Lord of all, to thee we raise This our hymn of grateful praise.

For thy Church that evermore Lifteth holy hands above,
Offering up on every shore Her pure sacrifice of love,
Lord of all, to thee we raise This our hymn of grateful praise.

Other prayers of thanksgiving can be found in poetry and
books on prayer.

All praise to God who now has turned
My fears to joys, my sighs to song,
My tears to smiles, my sad to glad. Amen.

Anne Bradstreet

✻

You have given so much to me,
Give one thing more, a grateful heart.

George Herbert

✳

We thank you for the triumph of truth over error, to us so slow, to yourself so sure. We bless you for every word of truth which has been spoken the wide world through, for all of right which human consciences have perceived and made into institutions.

We thank you for that love which will not stay its hold till it joins all nations and kindreds and tongues and people into one great family of love.

Theodore Parker

Dedication and Commitment

The story of salvation history is the story of God's great, steadfast love for us. Many of us, however, are fickle lovers who sometimes dedicate ourselves to loving and improving our relationship with God. At other times, we want nothing to do with God. We want to go it alone. We do not want to be encumbered by considerations of God and the doing of God's will*.

If we are sincere in teaching our children to love God, to be in relationship with God and to live according to God's will, it is important that we also teach our children to verbalize and, in fact, make a commitment to their relationship with God. Therefore, prayers of dedication and commitment are important. They help young people recall their relationship with God. They help give them a divine vision of life and of what is right and wrong. These prayers help maintain a high moral standard for their lives. They prevent them from succumbing to attractive temptations that exist all around them. Prayers of commitment and dedication keep our sacred garden of love for God free of weeds that can choke, strangle, or sap the strength from our growing children.

The Bible is full of statements and prayers of dedication and commitment. Some of these prayers follow.

When I think of your ways, I turn my feet to your decrees;
I hurry and do not delay to keep your commandments.
Though the cords of the wicked ensnare me,
    I do not forget your law.
At midnight I rise to praise you,
    because of your righteous ordinances.
I am a companion of all who stand in awe of you,
    of those who keep your precepts.
The earth, O Lord, is full of your steadfast love;
    teach me your statutes.

Psalm 119:59-64

✻

Praise the Lord!
Praise the Lord, O my soul!
I will praise the Lord as long as I live;
I will sing praises to my God all my life long.

Do not put your trust in princes, in mortals,
    in whom there is no help.
When their breath departs, they return to the earth;
    on that very day their plans perish.

Psalm 146:1-4

✻

But I will sing of your might;
I will sing aloud of your steadfast love in the morning.
For you have been a fortress for me
    and a refuge in the day of my distress.
O my strength, I will sing praises to you,
    for you, O God, are my fortress,
        the God who shows me steadfast love.

Psalm 59:16-17

Then I heard the voice of the Lord saying, "Whom shall I send, and who will go for us?" And I said, "Here am I; send me!"

Isaiah 6:8

✳

No slave can serve two masters; for a slave will either hate the one and love the other, or be devoted to the one and despise the other. You cannot serve God and wealth.

Luke 16:13

✳

I appeal to you therefore, brothers and sisters, by the mercies of God to present your bodies as a living sacrifice, holy and acceptable to God, which is your spiritual worship. Do not be conformed to this world, but be transformed by the renewing of your minds, so that you may discern what is the will of God—what is good and acceptable and perfect.

Romans 12:1-2

✳

Little children, let us love, not in word or speech, but in truth and action. And by this we will know that we are from the truth and will reassure our hearts before God whenever our hearts condemn us; for God is greater than our hearts, and God knows everything. Beloved, if our hearts do not condemn us, we have boldness before God; and we receive from God whatever we ask, because we obey God's commandments and do what pleases God.

And this is God's commandment, that we should believe in the name of Jesus Christ and love one another, just as he has commanded us. All who obey his commandments abide in him, and he abides in them. And by this we know that he abides in us, by the Spirit that he has given us.

I John 3:18-24

Our church hymnals have many hymns dedicated to the consecration of our lives to God.

Lord, Speak to Me, That I May Speak

Lord, speak to me, that I may speak
In living echoes of your tone;
As you have sought, so let me seek
Your erring children lost and lone.

O strengthen me, that while I stand
Firm on the rock, and strong in you,
I may stretch out a loving hand
To wrestlers with the troubled sea!

O teach me, Lord, that I may teach
The precious things you do impart;
And wing my words, that they may reach
The hidden depths of many a heart!

O fill me with your fullness, Lord,
Until my very heart o'erflow
In kindling thought and glowing word,
Your love to tell, your praise to show! Amen.

✳

God in Heaven, Who Lovest All

God in heaven, who lovest all,
O help your children when they call,
That they may build from age to age
An undefiled heritage.

Teach us to bear the yoke in youth,
With steadfastness and careful truth,
That, in our time, thy grace may give
The truth whereby the nations live.

Teach us to rule ourselves alway,
Controlled and cleanly night and day,
That we may bring, if need arise,
No maimed or worthless sacrifice.

Teach us to look in all our ends
On thee for judge and not our friends,
That we, with you, may walk uncowed
By fear or favor of the crowd.

Teach us the strength that cannot seek,
By deed or thought, to hurt the weak,
That under you, we may possess
Our strength to comfort other's distress.

Teach us delight in simple things,
And mirth that has no bitter springs,
Forgiveness free of evil done,
And love to all men 'neath the sun. Amen.

Rudyard Kipling

*

Take My Life and Let It Be

Take my life, and let it be
Consecrated, Lord, to thee;
Take my moments and my days,
Let them flow in ceaseless praise.

Take my hands, and let them move
At the impulse of your love;
Take my feet, and let them be
Swift and beautiful for thee;

Take my will, and make it thine;
It shall be no longer mine;
Take my heart, it is thine own;
It shall be thy royal throne.

Take my love: my Lord I pour
At your feet its treasure store;
Take myself, and I will be
Ever, only, all for thee. Amen.

Books on prayer also contain many prayers of dedication and commitment.

Jesus, wherever your people meet,
There they behold your mercy seat;
Wherever they seek you,
You are found,
And every place is hallowed ground.

For you, within no walls confined,
Inhabitest the humble mind;
You go where they go,
And going they take you to their home.

Great Shepherd of your chosen few
Your former mercies here renew;
Here to our waiting hearts proclaim

The sweetness of your saving name.
Here may we prove the power of prayer
To strengthen faith and sweeten care,
To teach our fain desires to rise,
And bring all heaven before our eyes. Amen.

William Cowper (variation)

✻

Creator God, into your hands I give my heart
Which left you but to learn how good you are.
George MacDonald (variation)

❋

God be in my head, And in my understanding;
God be in mine eyes, And in my looking;
God be in my mouth, And in my speaking;
God be in my heart, And in my thinking;
God be at mine end, And at my departing.
Sarum Primer

❋

Lord, take my heart, for I cannot give it to you. And when you
have it, keep it, for I would not take it from you. And save me
in spite of myself, for Christ's sake.
François de Salignac de La Mothe-Fenelon

❋

Almighty God, you who have made all things for us, and us
for your glory, sanctify our body and soul, our thoughts and
our intentions, our words and actions, that whatsoever we
shall think, or speak, or do, may by us be designed to the glori-
fication of your name...and let no pride or self-seeking, no impure motive or unworthy purpose, no little ends or low imagination stain our spirit, or profane any of our words and
actions. But let our body be a servant to our spirit, and both
body and spirit servants of Jesus Christ.
Thomas à Kempis

It is not so difficult for young people to take any of the above prayers as guides in formulating their own prayers of dedication and commitment. An overriding thought in dedicating one's life to God should be *Thy will be done, on earth as it is in heaven.*

O God, you have given me everything.
Through Jesus you have shown me
The Way, the Truth, and Life Eternal.
Jesus' love fills my heart.
His love helps me learn right from wrong.
His love creates a protective shield from
    the erring ways of other people.
Through the coming years,
I pledge my head, heart, and hands to you. Amen.

A.E.K.

*

O Lord, Jesus, you are my vision of what I can become.
Your wisdom and your life transcend earthly riches
    and people's praises.
All I ask is your presence and guidance
    as I journey through life.
I dedicate all that I am and all that I might become
    to your glory. Amen.

A.E.K.

Confession and Penitence

God loves us unconditionally. Most of us try to live according to God's will* but we and our children fall short of living it in thought, word and deed. Children learn at an early age their shortcomings. They may not be the best in sports, music, or in school. They may not be the best looking, the best speaker, the funniest person, and so on. We adults tend to push them to achieve great things. We forget they are children. We forget that failure is an important part of learning how to survive in life. When our children seemingly fail, we see that failure as our failure. We take it personally. Our reaction to their seeming failure gives some of them a sense of guilt. Many children have too much guilt and fear for their own good. They need to know that it is all right to fail, to try again, and to fail again. They need to know that God and we love them unconditionally. We are imperfect and so are they. Yet God has given us certain gifts with which to negotiate life. We need to encourage children to think positively. A damaged psyche harms them and prevents them from using effectively those gifts they have been given. Children need to be affirmed and empowered.

Confession and penitence help children and us to acknowledge our shortcomings and those sins we have committed as well as give us an opportunity for a fresh start. Confession is good for the soul, our psyche, and our relationship with God and each other.

Governing all our thoughts on confession should be the Lord's Prayer petition of "And forgive us our debts, as we forgive our debtors." (Refer to Chapter 6.)

There are two dangers our children face in confession. The first is the belief in "cheap grace." That is, they may take their sins too lightly and have no remorse for the sins they have committed against God and others. True confession must be sincere. If they make no amends for their sins and do not reform their ways, no spiritual regeneration happens. For true contrition to occur, young people need to be like the prodigal son who took responsibility for his actions, experienced the "far country," and returned home a wiser and more humble person.

The second danger our young people may have regarding confession is that they do not believe they are forgiven. Because guilt is so engrained in our society, they may indulge in morbid self-pity and self-examination which can adversely affect their mental state. For these young people, it is critical they understand that God's forgiveness for a particular act is once and for all. God's forgiveness cleanses them and restores their relationship with God. No matter what happens, they are loved by God even though their actions are not.

Everyone who wants God's forgiveness also must forgive those who have sinned against them. Joseph in the Old Testament and Jesus in the New Testament are good examples of people who forgave those who sought to destroy them. Many of us need to forgive God as well for not making life easy for us and the way we want it to be.

As stated in Chapter 11, children view life from their personal needs and desires. They learn rules and permissible behavior from parents and others. Sometimes our actions can distort distinctions for them. All of us without exception have need of God's mercy and compassion. In our churches, we come as one body to confess our sins to God. We have a General Confession that is the sum of our particular confessions. The General Confession should allow time for individuals to make their particular confessions as well. Children's confessions can be made during the General Confession during worship. One General Confession used in many churches goes as follows:

Most merciful God,
we confess that we have sinned against you
in thought, word, and deed,
by what we have done,
and by what we have left undone.
We have not loved you with our whole heart;
we have not loved our neighbors as ourselves.
We are truly sorry and we humbly repent.
For the sake of your Son Jesus Christ,
have mercy on us and forgive us;
that we may delight in your will,
and walk in your ways,
to the glory of your Name. Amen.

Book of Common Prayer

Two important features in this General Confession that young people may overlook are our sins of omission and our love of neighbor. Discuss both features with them.

The concept of sins of omission may be new to them. Give examples. Does a sin of omission mean that even though people do not deliberately commit an evil act they are morally held accountable for failure to act on someone's behalf?

For example, a young person may see his best friend steal something from the store in which he works. By failing to tell his friend to return the stolen item to the shelf or by failing to tell his employer, will that young person also be guilty of stealing? Or what about adults who get a cheaper entrance fee for their children because they claim they are younger than they actually are? And is it all right to lie by omission in order not to harm someone's feelings?

Young children

Prayers of confession are easy for young people to create because they come out of their own experience. *Very young children* need to ask God and those they offend almost immediately for forgiveness. If they do not, their sin will soon be forgotten and no sense of responsibility for their actions will develop. When they have done wrong, teach them to say a simple prayer of confession. Here are two that I wrote.

Dear God, forgive me for hurting _____.
I was mad at him and wanted to hurt him.
Help me to be good and not to hurt _____. Amen.

✻

Jesus, I love you.
But I did a terrible thing today.
I broke my sister's doll's head.
I told her I was sorry.
But she is still angry with me.
Forgive me.
Help her to forgive me.
Help me to do better next time. Amen.

Older Children and Adolescents

Older children and adolescents can make their specific confessions along the lines of these sample prayers.

I confess to you, Almighty and redeeming God,
    my indifference, my lack of faith
    and failure to live a pure, holy life.
I trust too much in things and people and not in you.
I use my blessings to my advantage over others
    rather than to share them with them.
I fail to treat people as my brother or sister whom you love.
Forgive me for my self-centeredness
    and the sins that grow out of this self-centeredness.
Help me to live a more Christ-like life.
Help me to withstand distracting temptations
    and to let your will control my life. Amen.

A.E.K.

✳

Almighty and merciful God, help me!
The anger I feel towards my parents grows daily.
It does not help our relationship either.
I know they only want the best for me.
But somehow I cannot stand their constant meddling.
Then I lose my temper and say things to hurt them.
Sometimes they do not understand my problems.
They make hasty and harmful judgments.
However, it is heartless of me to hurt them.
The next time they interfere in my affairs,
    help them and me to govern our tempers and anxieties.
Help us begin a dialogue rather than
    continue our shouting match.
Help each of us to disagree peaceably
    when there is a difference of opinion.
Help us to respect each other's point of view.
Help us to live according to your will*.
May we have your peace*. Amen.

A.E.K.

Dear Jesus, my Creator, Redeemer, and Sustainer,
   help me govern my body and the emotions I feel.
You have given me a sexual drive which is a natural part of me.
Help me to know when it is right to share my sexuality.
Help me to turn my sexual energy into something positive.
Help me to do what is right and not to give in to lust. Amen.

A.E.K.

*

O God, I know you love me and your love should be sufficient.
But somehow envy takes over my thoughts
   and controls my actions.
How I envy M.J. It seems she never does anything wrong.
She is not clumsy like me. Her hair is always perfect,
   and her skin is free of pimples.
Did Jesus have pimples and was He clumsy?
I am like an awkward ugly duckling next to M.J.
Everybody loves her and only tolerates me. What am I to do?
I know I should not be envious or jealous, but I am.
Forgive me for breaking your commandment
   to love one another.
Help me not to compare myself with others.
Help me to use the gifts you have given me in your work,
   and may all I think and do be for your glory. Amen.

A.E.K.

*

O wonderful Jesus,
    you came into this world to free us from our sins.
My actions make a sacrilege of your sacrifice.
Not only have I sinned against you,
    but I sinned against _____ in thought, word, and deed.
He is very hurt and will not speak to me or forgive me.
Will you forgive me?
You said you would forgive those
    who are truly sorry for their sins.
I am truly sorry for my sins. Please forgive me.
Let me know that I am forgiven. Help me to do what is right.
Help me not to misuse the blessings
    you have given me. Amen.

A.E.K.

The Bible includes people's personal confessions and talks about God's forgiveness. For instance, the prodigal son resolved to say to his father:

Father, I have sinned against heaven and before you; I am no longer worthy to be called your son; treat me like one of your hired hands.

Luke 15:18

When his father saw him approaching home from afar, the father dropped all decorum and rushed down the road to meet and embrace his beloved and once wayward son. The father welcomed his son home and said: "for this son of mine was dead and is alive again; he was lost and is found" (Luke 15:24).

*

Paul tells King Agrippa of his evil deeds against Christians, of his conversion, and of his missionary work. He said:

When we had all fallen to the ground, I heard a voice saying to me..."Saul, Saul, why are you persecuting me?"....I asked, "Who are you, Lord?" The Lord answered, "I am Jesus whom you are persecuting. But get up and stand on your feet; for I have appeared to you for this purpose, to appoint you to serve and testify to the things in which you have seen me and to those in which I will appear to you. I will rescue you from your people and from the Gentiles—to whom I am sending you to open their eyes so that they may turn from darkness to light and from the power of Satan to God, so that they may receive forgiveness of sins and a place among those who are sanctified by faith in me."

Acts 26:14-18

*

The prophet Isaiah had a vision of God in the Temple. He said:

"Woe is me! I am lost, for I am a man of unclean lips, and I live among a people of unclean lips; yet my eyes have seen the King, the Lord of hosts!"

Then one of the seraphs flew to me, holding a live coal that had been taken from the altar with a pair of tongs. The seraph touched my mouth with it and said: "Now that this has touched your lips, your guilt has departed and your sin is blotted out."

Isaiah 6:5-7

After Isaiah is cleansed of his sin, he committed the rest of his life as God's prophet.

The prophet Ezekiel talks about God's forgiveness when he says:

But if the wicked turn away from all their sins that they have committed and keep all my statutes and do what is lawful and right, they shall surely live; they shall not die. None of the transgressions that they have committed shall be remembered against them; for the righteousness that they have done they shall live.

Ezekiel 18:21-22

*

Jesus instructed His disciples about forgiveness when he said:

I have come to call not the righteous but sinners to repentance.

Luke 5:32

*

Be on your guard! If another disciple sins, you must rebuke the offender, and if there is repentance, you must forgive. And if the same person sins against you seven times a day, and turns back to you seven times and says, "I repent," you must forgive.

Luke 17:3-4

*

The apostle Paul said:

Now I rejoice, not because you were grieved, but because your grief led to repentance; for you felt a godly grief, so that you were not harmed in any way by us. For godly grief produces a repentance that leads to salvation and brings no regret, but worldly grief produces death.

I Corinthians 7:9-10

Hymns of confession are also a good guide in helping people think about making their confession. John Wesley wrote the following hymn.

O Thou to Whose All Searching Sight

O thou to whose all searching sight
The darkness shineth as the light,
Search, prove my heart; it longs for thee;
O burst these bonds, and set it free!

Wash out its stains, refine its dross,
Nail my affections to the cross;
Hallow each thought; let all within
Be clean, as thou, my Lord, art clean.

If in this darksome wild I stray,
Be thou my light, be thou my way;
No foes, no evils need I fear,
No harm, while thou, my God, art near.

Savior, wher-e'er thy steps I see,
Dauntless, untired, I follow thee.
O let thy hand support me still,
And lead me to thy holy hill! Amen.

✳

Prayers by other people found in various books on prayer can be helpful, too. Thomas à Kempis acknowledges our humanness when he wrote:

And I offer also for all those whom I have in any way grieved, vexed, oppressed, and scandalized, by word or deed, knowingly or unknowingly; that thou mayest equally forgive us all our sins, and all our offenses against each other.

Take away, O Lord, from our hearts all suspiciousness, indignation, anger, and contention, and whatever is calculated to wound charity, and to lessen brotherly love.

Have mercy, O Lord, have mercy on those who seek thy mercy; give grace to the needy; make us so to live, that we may be found worthy to enjoy the fruition of thy grace, and that we may attain to eternal life.

Psalm 51 is a great penitential prayer asking God for moral health and spiritual renewal. It ends with a commitment to praise and serve God. A few verses of this psalm follow.

Have mercy on me, O God, according to your steadfast love;
    according to your abundant mercy
    blot out my transgressions.
Wash me thoroughly from my iniquity,
    and cleanse me from my sin.

For I know my transgressions, and my sin is ever before me.
Against you, you alone, have I sinned,
    and done what is evil in your sight....

You desire truth in the inward being;
    therefore teach me wisdom in my secret heart.
Purge me with hyssop, and I shall be clean;
    wash me, and I shall be whiter than snow....

O Lord, open my lips, and my mouth will declare your praise.
For you have no delight in sacrifice....

The sacrifice acceptable to God is a broken spirit;
    a broken and contrite heart, O God you will not despise.

Psalm 51:1-4, 6-7, 15-17

Use any or all of the preceding prayers as models to help your children create their own prayers of confession. Other prayers of confession not covered here could be on such topics as greed, laziness, lying, cheating, misrepresentation, substance abuse, damage or destruction of other people's property, self indulgence, discrimination, racial injustice, pride, and the like.

After people make their confessions, people need to be reminded of God's forgiveness with some words of assurance. Words of assurance for the forgiveness of our sins are found throughout the Bible. Some words of assurance are as follows:

Remember these things, O people.
    You will not be forgotten by me.
I have swept away your transgressions like a cloud,
        and your sins like mist;
        return to me, for I have redeemed you.

Isaiah 44:21-22

✻

For God so loved the world that he gave his only Son, so that everyone who believes in him may not perish but may have eternal life.

John 3:16

Variations on biblical words of assurance convey a reassuring word that God forgives our sins.

We, who are in Christ, are a new creation.
The old has passed away.
Everything has become new.
God entrusts us to spread God's message of reconciliation.
Thanks be to God! Amen.

2 Corinthians 5:16-21 (Variation)

✻

Christ Jesus came into the world to save sinners,
to free us from the enslaving bonds of sin,
to free us to love God and neighbor
so that we may become what we were meant to be.
Thanks be to God. Amen.

1 Timothy 1:15 (Variation)

✳

God forgives us and does not remind us of our past sins.
Let us live as free, obedient Christians. Amen.

A.E.K.

Blessing

Most blessings identified in the Bible are gifts from God. Abraham was considered to be blessed by God. In Genesis 12, this blessing is explained in greater detail.

Now the Lord said to Abram, "Go from your country and your kindred and your father's house to the land that I will show you. And I will make of you a great nation, and I will bless you, and make your name great, so that you will be a blessing. I will bless those who bless you, and the one who curses you I will curse; and in you all the families of the earth shall be blessed."

Genesis 12:1-3

God is promising Abraham three very important things. The first promise is land for him and his descendants. The second promise is a great nation formed from his seed. And the last promise is that through him blessings will be mediated to other people.

For this reason, Isaac's blessing on Jacob was considered worth more than any material goods. It is almost as though holy power is being transferred to the person receiving the blessing. Isaac blessed Jacob with these words:

May God give you of the dew of heaven,
    and of the fatness of the earth, and plenty of grain and wine.
Let peoples serve you, and nations bow down to you.
Be lord over your brothers,
    and may your mother's sons bow down to you.
Cursed be every one who curses you,
    and blessed be every one who blesses you!

Genesis 27:28-29

Rain, fertility, domination, and superiority over others are contained within this blessing. From Jacob this blessing seems to be carried forward by his beloved son, Joseph. Those people associated with Joseph are either blessed or cursed according to their treatment of him. People in early Old Testament times believed success went with the person who carried God's blessing.

Another Old Testament blessing along these lines is found in Deuteronomy 30. Here Moses asked his people to choose between life and death. By life, Moses meant love and obedience to God. Moses said:

I call heaven and earth to witness against you today that I have set before you life and death, blessings and curses. Choose life so that you and your descendants may live, loving the Lord your God, obeying him, and holding fast to him; for that means life to you and length of days, so that you may live in the land that the Lord swore to give to your ancestors, to Abraham, to Isaac, and to Jacob.

Deuteronomy 30:19-20

This theme continues throughout many of the psalms. Psalm 24 defines who will receive God's blessing.

Who shall ascend the hill of the Lord?
  And who shall stand in his holy place?
Those who have clean hands and pure hearts,
    who do not lift up their souls to what is false,
    and do not swear deceitfully.
They will receive blessing from the Lord,
    and vindication from the God of salvation.

Psalm 24:3-5

Matthew's gospel was written from a Jewish Christian point of view for the conversion of the Jewish people. He emphasized Jesus as the fulfillment of the Old Testament prophecies in order to convince the Jewish people that Jesus is the Messiah. Matthew's gospel is also more Jewish than the other gospels. There is an emphasis on keeping the Law of Moses as a Christian duty to God. For these reasons, the Old Testament concept of blessings is carried forward in his gospel. The best example of receiving God's blessing is found in the Sermon on the Mount (Matthew 5). Another example goes as follows:

Therefore, I tell you, do not worry about your life, what you will eat or what you will drink, or about your body, what you will wear. Is not life more than food, and the body more than clothing?....Therefore, do not worry, saying, "What will we eat?" or "What will we wear?" For it is the Gentiles who strive for all these things; and indeed your heavenly Father knows that you need all these things. But strive first for the kingdom of God and his righteousness, and all these things will be given to you as well.

Matthew 6:25, 31-33

or

"Come, you that are blessed by my Father, inherit the king-dom prepared for you from the foundation of the world; for I was hungry and you gave me food, I was thirsty and you gave me something to drink, I was a stranger and you welcomed me"...."Lord, when was it that we saw you hungry and gave you food, or thirsty and gave you something to drink?"...."Truly I tell you, just as you did it to one of the least of these who are members of my family, you did it to me."

Matthew 25:34-40

In New Testament times and in our day, blessings are re-quests made to God for God to favor either certain people or some endeavor or something. Typical New Testament bless-ings along these lines are:

The grace of the Lord Jesus Christ, the love of God, and the communion of the Holy Spirit be with all of you. Amen.

2 Corinthians 13:13

✳

The peace of God, which passes all understanding,
    keep your hearts and minds
    in the knowledge and love of God,
    and of Christ Jesus our risen Savior.
And the blessing of God Almighty,
Creator, Redeemer, and Comforter,
    be among you and remain with you always. Amen.

Philippians 4:7

✳

May the God of hope fill you with all joy and peace in believ-ing, so that you may abound in hope by the power of the Holy Spirit. Amen.

Romans 15:13

✳

The grace of the Lord Jesus be with all the saints. Amen.

Revelation 22:21

People often ask their minister or priest to bless their children, animals, houses, boats, or some endeavor. Recently, I blessed a friend's boat. My blessing went something like this:

Dear God, maker of heaven and earth,
    please bless this craft. Keep it seaworthy.
Bless those who will be sailing it.
Let them have health and happiness
    in these their retirement years.
Give them courage, comfort, and strength
    to endure all life's storms.
May they keep a steady course and a cool head
    as they venture into the unknown and eventually come
    to their eternal rest with you. Amen.

A.E.K.

Blessings have become a part of today's liturgy. Most worship services close with a benediction wherein the minister or priest raises the right hand or makes the sign of the cross while saying the blessing. Non-scriptural based benedictions abound.

May God bless you with all good and keep you from all evil; may God give light to your heart with loving wisdom, and be gracious to you with eternal knowledge; may God lift up God's loving countenance upon you for eternal peace.

Dead Sea Scrolls

✳

The Lord Jesus Christ be near to defend you, within you to refresh you, around you to preserve you, before you to guide you, behind you to justify you, above you to bless you.

Anonymous

✳

May the road rise to meet you.
May the wind be always at your back.
May the sun shine warm upon your face.
May the rains fall softly upon your fields
And until we meet again
May God hold you in the hollow of his hand.

Gaelic Blessing

Listening

Many times I think God would rather have us be quiet in prayer and say nothing. Prayer is often wordless and is a form of intense listening to the word of God found in scripture, sacred music, poetry, other people's prayers, and in what other people have to say and do. Sometimes we and our children are meant to be silent listeners and observers in our communication with God. Jesus said:

Everyone then who hears these words of mine and acts on them will be like a wise man who built his house on rock. The rain fell, the floods came, and the winds blew and beat on that house, but it did not fall, because it had been founded on rock. And everyone who hears these words of mine and does not act on them will be like a foolish man who built his house on sand. The rain fell, and the floods came, and the winds blew and beat against that house, and it fell—and great was its fall!

Matthew 7:24-27

Let me conclude this book with my prayer for you and the children in your care.

The Spirit of God broods over our earth.
The Spirit of God seeks our company and our love
    and walks abroad.
The Spirit of God blows where it will—
    through the trees, over the waters, and round about us.
Can we not feel it? Can we not sense it?
Can we not know it? Can we not hear it?

God whispers to us:
    "Come unto me all you who are weary and heavy laden,
    and I will give you peace....Be still and learn of me.
    Know that I am God, your Creator.
    Let me be your friend and comforter.
    Love me, believe in me, speak to me,
        listen to me, and do my will.
    Then I will always be present to you,
        to encourage you when you are discouraged,
        to give you spiritual strength when you are tempted,
        to disperse the darkness that causes you to stumble,
        to give you a light to travel an unknown path,
        to give you hope when all appears hopeless,
        to give you faith when doubt begins to overtake you,
        to teach you to practice mercy, justice, and kindness
        in my name to all who come your way
        until you make your final journey to my eternal home."

Spirit of God, make us One with You. Amen.

Notes

*

1. James Hastings, D.D., ed., *The Christian Doctrine of Prayer* (New York: Charles Scribner's Sons, 1915), pp. 341-42.

2. Robert Coles, *The Spiritual Life of Children* (Boston: Houghton Mifflin Company, 1990), p. 49.

3. Bill Huebsch, *A New Look at Prayer* (Mystic, CT: Twenty-Third Publications, 1991), p. 6.

4. Hastings, p. 340.

5. Ibid., p. 345.

6. Ibid., p. 208.

7. Coles, p. 60-61.

8. Ibid., p. 26-27.

9. Ibid., p. 27.

10. Ibid.

11. James Carse, *The Silence of God* (New York: Macmillan Publishing Company, 1985), p. 15.

12. Harry Emerson Fosdick, *The Meaning of Prayer* (Nashville: Abingdon Press, 1984) pp. 81-82.

13. Ibid., p. 82.

14. Carse, p. 21.

15. Bernard Lohse, *A Short History of Christian Doctrine*. Translated by F. Ernest Stoeffler (Philadelphia: Fortress Press, 1980), p. 68.

16. Laurel Friedmann.

17. Known as the "Dougy Letter." If you or someone you know has a child who is dying, I recommend that this child be given this letter. You can get it by writing Elisabeth Kubler-Ross, M.D., South Route 616, Head Waters, VA 24442.

18. Ibid.

19. Webster's New World Dictionary.

20. Fredrich Heiler, *Prayer, A Study in the History of Religion*, translated by Samuel McComb (New York: Oxford University Press, 1932), p. 88.

21. Marguerite Shuster, *Power Pathology, Paradox, The Dynamics of Evil and Good* (Grand Rapids: Academie Books, 1987), p. 21.

22. Ibid., p. 73.

23. Ibid., pp. 165-66.

24. Ibid., p. 172.

25. Joseph Stein, *Fiddler on the Roof* (New York: Crown Publishers, Inc., 1964), p. 18.

26. Ibid., p. 33.

27. Heiler, p. 170.

28. Hastings, p. 96.

29. Ibid., p. 10.

Glossary

*

Doxology—Words of praise to God.

God's Will—Unity, peace, wholeness, joy, goodness, righteousness, purity, fidelity, love, hope, and faithfulness.

Hallowed—holy. Something that is holy is set apart, considered sacred and regarded with awe.

Heaven—any place where we experience God's presence.

Kingdom of God—any place where people live according to God's will. It has its start on earth and its completion in heaven.

Shalom or **Peace**—freedom from internal and external conflict and from unjust barriers between people. *Shalom* is the experience of God's grace and tranquility of heart.

Bibliography

*

Appleton, George., ed. *The Oxford Book of Prayer.* New York: Oxford Univesity Press, 1985.

Barclay, William. *A Barclay Prayer Book.* Philadelphia: Trinity Press International, 1990.

Baycroft, John. *The Way of Prayer.* Toronto: Anglican Book Centre, 1983.

Carse, James P. *The Silence of God.* New York: Macmillan Publishing Company, 1985.

Coles, Robert. *The Spiritual Life of Children.* Boston: Houghton Mifflin Company, 1990.

Davies, Horton. ed. *The Communion of Saints.* Grand Rapids: William B. Eerdmans Publishing Company, 1990.

Duck, Ruth C. and Bausch, Michael G., ed. *Everflowing Streams, Songs for Worship.* New York: Pilgrim Press, 1986.

Fackre, Dorothy and Gabriel. *Christian Basics, A Primer for Pilgrims.* Grand Rapids: William B. Eerdmans Publishing Company, 1991.

Fackre, Gabriel. *The Christian Story.* Grand Rapids: William B. Eerdmans Publishing Company, 1984.

Gasztold, Carmen Bernos de. *Prayers from the Ark and the Creatures' Choir.* Translated by Rumer Godden. New York: Penguin Books, 1976.

Hall, Douglas John. *When You Pray.* Valley Forge: Judson Press, 1987.

Huebsch, Bill. *A New Look at Prayer, Searching for Bliss*. Mystic, CT: Twenty-Third Publications, 1991.

Lochman, Jan Milc. *The Lord's Prayer*. Translated by Geoffrey W. Bromiley. Grand Rapids: William B. Eerdmans Publishing Company, 1990.

Ng, David and Thomas, Virginia. *Children in the Worshiping Community*. Atlanta: John Knox Press, 1981.

LeFevre, Perry. *Understandings of Prayer*. Philadelphia: The Westminster Press, 1981.

Nagel, Myra B. *Talking With Your Child About Prayer*. New York: United Church Press, 1990.

Nouwen, Henri J. M. *With Open Hands*. Notre Dame: Ave Maria Press, 1982.

Quoist, Michel. *New Prayers*. Translated by Elizabeth Lovatt-Dolan. New York: Crossroad, 1992.

Quoist, Michel. *Prayers*. Translated by Agnes M. Forsyth and Anne Marie de Commaille. Kansas City: Sheed Andrews and McMeel, 1963.

Roberts, Elizabeth and Amidon, Elias, ed. *Earth Prayers*. San Francisco: Harper SanFrancisco, 1991.

Simon, Mary Manz. *God's Children Pray*. St. Louis: Concordia Publishing House, 1989.

Smith, Martin L. *The Word Is Very Near You*. Cambridge: Cowley Publications, 1989.

Stott, Joan, ed. *In God's Presence, prayers, poems, and praise for devotions*. Melbourne: The Joint Board of Christian Education, 1989.

Sydnor, William. *More Than Words*. San Francisco: Harper and Row, Publishers, 1990.

Weems, Ann. *Searching for Shalom*. Louisville: Westminster/ John Knox Press, 1991.

Winter, Miriam Therese. *An Anthology of Scripture Songs*. Philadelphia: Medical Mission Sisters, 1982.